LawExpress

BUSINESS LAW

LawExpress

BUSINESS LAW

4th edition

Ewan MacIntyre
Senior Lecturer in Law at Nottingham Trent University

PEARSON

Harlow, England • London • New York • Boston • San Francisco • Toronto • Sydney • Auckland • Singapore • Hong Kong
Tokyo • Seoul • Taipei • New Delhi • Cape Town • São Paulo • Mexico City • Madrid • Amsterdam • Munich • Paris • Milan

Pearson Education Limited
Edinburgh Gate
Harlow
Essex CM20 2JE
England
and Associated Companies throughout the world.

Visit us on the World Wide Web at:
www.pearson.com/uk

First published 2008 (print)
Second edition 2010 (print)
Third edition published 2013 (print)
Fourth edition published 2015 (print and electronic)

ISBN: 978-1-292-01290-2 (print)
978-1-292-01340-4 (PDF)
978-1-292-01308-4 (eText)
978-1-292-01810-2 (ePub)

British Library Cataloguing-in-Publication Data
A catalogue record for the print edition is available from the British Library

Library of Congress Cataloging-in-Publication Data
A catalog record for this book is available from the Library of Congress

10 9 8 7 6 5 4 3 2 1
17 16 15 14

Print edition typeset in 10/12pt Helvetica Neue LT Std by 35
Print edition printed and bound in Malaysia (CTP-PPSB)

NOTE THAT ANY PAGE CROSS REFERENCES REFER TO THE PRINT EDITION

Contents

Supporting resources

Visit the *Law Express* series companion website at **www.pearsoned.co.uk/lawexpress** to find valuable student learning material including:

- A **study plan** test to help you assess how well you know the subject before you begin your revision
- Interactive **quizzes** to test your knowledge of the main points from each chapter
- Sample **examination questions** and guidelines for answering them
- Interactive **flashcards** to help you revise key terms, cases and statutes
- Printable versions of the **topic maps** and **checklists** from the book
- **'You be the marker'** allows you to see exam questions and answers from the perspective of the examiner and includes notes on how an answer might be marked
- **Podcasts** provide point-by-point instruction on how to answer a typical exam question

Also: The companion website provides the following features:

- Search tool to help locate specific items of content
- E-mail results and profile tools to send results of quizzes to instructors
- Online help and support to assist with website usage and troubleshooting

For more information please contact your local Pearson Education sales representative or visit **www.pearsoned.co.uk/lawexpress**

Acknowledgements

I would like to thank Zoe Botterill for her frequent suggestions as to how the text could be improved.

Ewan MacIntyre

Publisher's acknowledgements

Our thanks go to all reviewers who contributed to the development of this text, including students who participated in research and focus groups which helped to shape the series format.

Introduction

Generally, a business law exam would contain more problem questions than essay questions. For many students of business law this is the only law exam they will ever take. Perhaps for this reason, problem questions are not always answered well.

Above all, problem questions require you to apply the law to the question set. This book is a revision guide, not a substitute for a textbook or course notes. It sets out the important principles of law clearly, so that you can see the framework of the subject and can also see what is important and what is not. Clearly understanding this framework will improve your problem answering technique in several ways. First of all, you will have a solid overview of the subject, so that when you are faced with a problem question you will be able to see what the question is about. Next, you will understand the main principles which will be relevant to the problem question set, and so you will be able to explain those principles when answering the question. Finally, you will understand the context of the main principles which you apply to the problem question. You will see how these principles apply in conjunction with other principles relating to other subjects. Despite these advantages, you should remember that to do really well you will also need the detail which is contained in your lecture notes or recommended textbook.

Even though the majority of questions in a business law exam are likely to be problem questions, there are also likely to be some essay questions. You will probably be more familiar with such questions, having previously answered similar questions in exams on other subjects. Again, this guide will help you to answer such questions because it will give you a clear overview of each topic. It will also let you see the relative importance of one area compared to another. This will allow your answer to show an awareness of the bigger picture, and an understanding of how the relevant topics relate to each other.

REVISION NOTE

- Revise with this book first to get a good overview of the subject, but remember that you will also need your course materials and recommended textbook.
- Demonstrate that you know how one topic interrelates with another.
- Use this book not only for revision but also to understand a subject as it is being covered on your course.
- Do not let problem questions fluster you just because you are not familiar with them. The first step is to see which area of law the question is about. This book will let you do that. It will also help you with the next step, actually applying the law.

Before you begin, you can use the study plan available on the companion website to assess how well you know the material in this book and identify the areas where you may want to focus your revision.

Guided tour

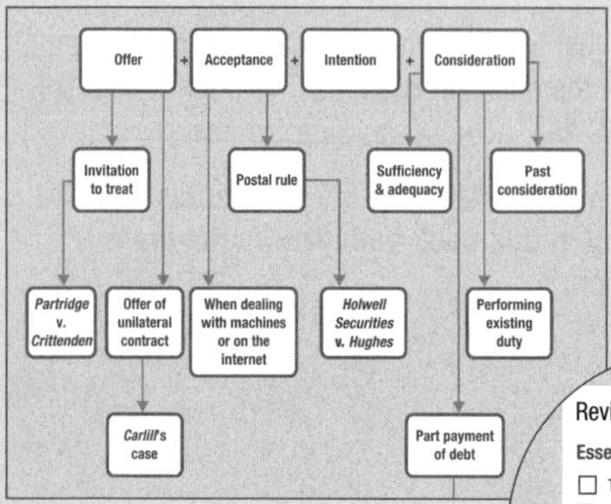

Topic maps – Visual guides highlight key subject areas and facilitate easy navigation through the chapter. Download them from the companion website to pin on your wall or add to your revision notes.

Revision checklists – How well do you know each topic? Use these to identify essential points you should know for your exams. But don't panic if you don't know them all – the chapters will help you revise each point to ensure you are fully prepared. Print the checklists off the companion website and track your revision progress!

Revision checklist

Essential points you should know

- ☐ The difference between an offer and ar
- ☐ How an acceptance is made and when a
- ☐ The presumptions which apply when co to create legal relations
- ☐ The definition of consideration, and the 'adequacy'
- ☐ The kinds of promises which canr

Sample questions with answer guidelines – Practice makes perfect! Read the question at the start of each chapter and consider how you would answer it. Guidance on structuring strong answers is provided at the end of the chapter. Try out additional sample questions online.

Sample question

Could you answer this question? Below is a typical problem question that could arise on this topic. Guidelines on answering the question are included at the end of this chapter, while a sample essay question and guidance on tackling it can be found on the companion website.

Assessment advice – Not sure how best to tackle a problem or essay question? Wondering what you may be asked? Use the assessment advice to identify the ways in which a subject may be examined and how to apply your knowledge effectively.

ASSESSMENT ADVICE

Essay questions

Essay questions on offer and acceptance are relatively uncommon. Essay questions on consideration are more commonly set. If there is such a question you must read it carefully. Does it require you to deal with consideration in general? If so, all of the rules relating to consideration will have to be dealt with. Or does the question relate only to certain aspects of consideration? If so, you should first define consideration and then confine your answer to the relevant subjects.

Problem questions

These are often based on only one or two of the requirements of a contract. For example, a question might be based almost wholly on offer and acceptance. Even so, intention and consideration are worth one line each. Without these there will be no contract. Again, some problem questions are primarily about consideration. When answering such questions, offer, acceptance and intention should be mentioned briefly. If they are not present, there will be no contract.

Key definitions – Make sure you understand essential legal terms. Use the flashcards online to test your recall!

KEY DEFINITION: Offeror and offeree

An offeror is a person who makes an offer.

An offeree is a person to whom an offer has been made.

Key cases and key statutes – Identify and review the important elements of the essential cases and statutes you will need to know for your exams.

> KEY STATUTE
>
> **Sale of Goods Act 1979,**
>
> Where there is a sale of go
> goods will correspond with
>
> This section is surprisingl
> ctually have been a d

> KEY CASE
>
> *Partridge* v. *Crittenden* [1968] 2 All ER 421 (Div Ct)
>
> ***Concerning: whether advertisements are usually offers or invitations to treat***
>
> **Facts**
>
> The defendant advertised wild birds for sale. A customer replied and had a bird sent to him. The defendant was charged with the criminal offence of 'offering for sale' a wild bird. The defendant was not guilty. He had not 'offered for sale' the wild bird.

Make your answer stand out – This feature illustrates sources of further thinking and debate where you can maximise your marks. Use them to really impress your examiners!

> ✓ Make your answer stand out
>
> Show that you know Denning J's explanation of promissory estoppel was not the *ratio decidendi* of the case. It was only *obiter dicta* (see p. 181) and therefore not strictly binding. You should be aware of the extent to which other cases support or discredit the idea of promissory estoppel. Answers which can thoughtfully compare these always get good grades.

Exam tips – Feeling the pressure? These boxes indicate how you can improve your exam performance when it really counts.

> EXAM TIP
>
> Many questions focus on whether or not an offer was still open at the time when it was accepted. Revocation of an offer is effective when it is received by the offeree. So these questions usually come down to analysing who communicated first. Was the offer revoked before it was accepted, in which case there is no contract? Or was it accepted before it was revoked, in which case a contract was formed? But don't forget that acceptance of an offer of a unilateral contract does not need to be communicated.

Revision notes – Get guidance for effective revision. These boxes highlight related points and areas of overlap in the subject, or areas where your course might adopt a particular approach that you should check with your course tutor.

> REVISION NOTE
>
> An answer which thoughtfully applies *Holwell Securities Ltd* v. *Hughes* is likely to get a good grade.
>
> Offer and acceptance when dealing with machines
>
> Goods are commonly bought from machines. So are tickets which entitle the owner to a service. Obviously, a contract is formed when such tickets are bought. The main reason for

Don't be tempted to . . . – This feature underlines areas where students most often trip up in exams. Use them to spot common pitfalls and avoid losing marks.

> ! Don't be tempted to . . .
>
> You should not apply the postal rule to acceptance of an offer by e-mail. There is as yet no precedent on the time at which an e-mail is received, for the purposes of acceptance and revocation. This makes the law in this area uncertain. However, it can be ascertained by applying some cases concerning communication by telex.

Read to impress – Focus on these carefully selected sources to extend your knowledge, deepen your understanding, and earn better marks in coursework as well as in exams.

> READ TO IMPRESS
>
> Blair, A. (1996) Minding Your Own Business – *Williams* v. *Roffey* Revisited: A Consideration Reconsidered, JBL 254–65
>
> Capps, D. (2004) Electronic Mail and the Postal Rule, 15(7) ICCLR 207–12
>
> Halson, R. (1999) The Offensive Limits of Promissory Estoppel, 2 LMCLQ 256–77

Glossary – Forgotten the meaning of a word? This quick reference covers key definitions and other useful terms.

> **Glossary of terms**
>
> The glossary is divided into two parts: key definitions and other useful terms. The key definitions can be found within the chapter in which they occur as well as in the glossary below. These definitions are the essential terms that you must know and understand in order to prepare for an exam. The additional list of terms provides further definitions of useful terms and phrases which will also help you answer examination and coursework questions effectively. These terms are highlighted in the text on their first occurrence but the definition can only be found here.

Guided tour of the companion website

Book resources are available to download. Print your own **topic maps** and **revision checklists**!

Use the **study plan** prior to your revision to help you assess how well you know the subject and determine which areas need most attention. Choose to take the full assessment or focus on targeted study units.

'Test your knowledge' of individual areas with quizzes tailored specifically to each chapter. **Sample problem and essay questions** are also available with guidance on writing a good answer.

Flashcards test and improve recall of important legal terms, key cases and statutes. Available in both electronic and printable formats.

'You be the marker' gives you the chance to evaluate sample exam answers for different question types and understand how and why an examiner awards marks.

Download the **podcast** and listen as your own personal Law Express tutor guides you through answering a typical but challenging question. A step-by-step explanation on how to approach the question is provided, including what essential elements your answer will need for a pass, how to structure a good response, and what to do to make your answer stand out so that you can earn extra marks.

All of this and more can be found when you visit **www.pearsoned.co.uk/lawexpress**

Table of cases and statutes

Cases

Statutes

Statutory Instruments

Contract 1:

Formation of a contract

Revision checklist

Essential points you should know:

- [ ] The difference between an offer and an invitation to treat
- [ ] How an acceptance is made and when an acceptance becomes effective
- [ ] The presumptions which apply when considering whether there was an intention to create legal relations
- [ ] The definition of consideration, and the meaning of both 'sufficiency' and 'adequacy'
- [ ] The kinds of promises which cannot amount to valid consideration

Topic map

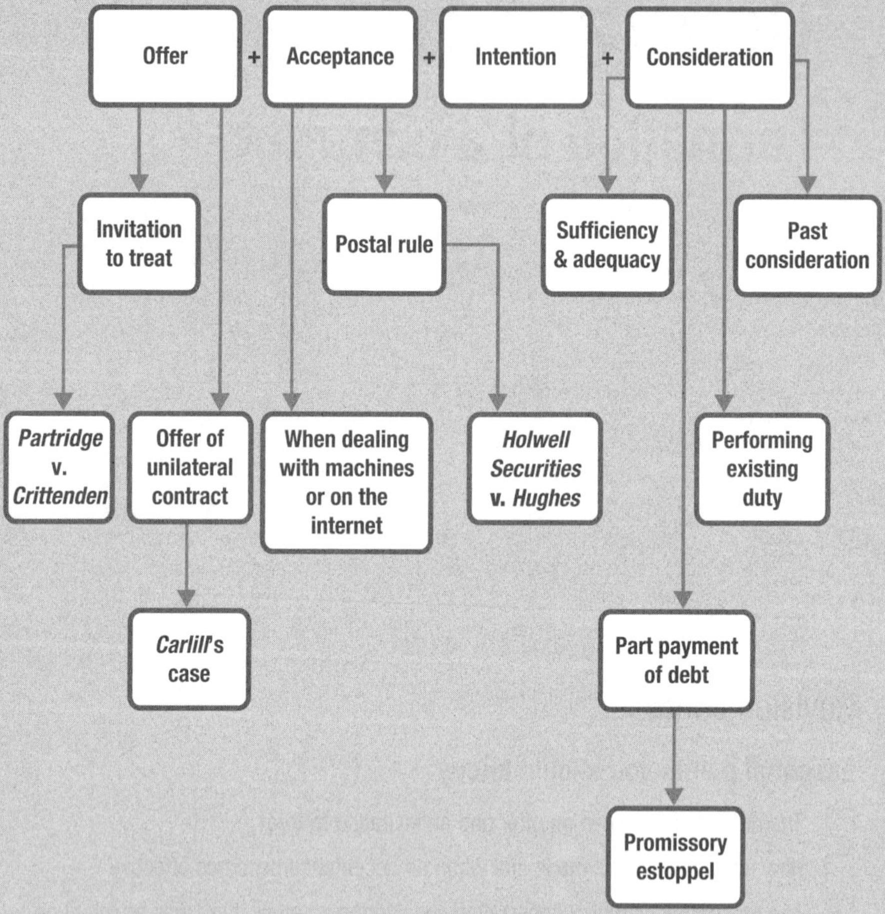

A printable version of this topic map is available from **www.pearsoned.co.uk/lawexpress**

Introduction

This is one of the most interesting areas of contract law and is a very common exam topic.

The law on offer and acceptance is made up of a series of rules which have evolved over the years. Taken together the rules make very good business sense and if you understand the sense of the rules it makes them easier to remember.

ASSESSMENT ADVICE

Essay questions

Essay questions on offer and acceptance are relatively uncommon. Essay questions on consideration are more commonly set. If there is such a question you must read it carefully. Does it require you to deal with consideration in general? If so, all of the rules relating to consideration will have to be dealt with. Or does the question relate only to certain aspects of consideration? If so, you should first define consideration and then confine your answer to the relevant subjects.

Problem questions

These are often based on only one or two of the requirements of a contract. For example, a question might be based almost wholly on offer and acceptance. Even so, intention and consideration are worth one line each. Without these there will be no contract. Again, some problem questions are primarily about consideration. When answering such questions, offer, acceptance and intention should be mentioned briefly. If they are not present, there will be no contract.

Sample question

Could you answer this question? Below is a typical problem question that could arise on this topic. Guidelines on answering the question are included at the end of this chapter, while a sample essay question and guidance on tackling it can be found on the companion website.

PROBLEM QUESTION

Huge Ltd, a large department store, advertise a price promise in a local newspaper. This states that if any customer buys from them and, within 28 days, notifies them in writing that the same goods are on sale at a lower price in another local shop they can have all of the purchase price returned to them. On 1 June Marc buys a camera from the store for £49.99. On 27 June Marc posts a letter, truthfully explaining that the same camera is on sale at another shop for £49.89. Marc's letter arrives on 30 June. Marc insists that he is entitled to all of his money back but Huge Ltd refuse to refund any of the purchase price.

Advise Marc as to whether or not he has a contractual right to have the purchase price returned.

Offer

There is no statutory or universally recognised definition, but an offer might be defined as 'a proposition put by one person (the **offeror**) to another person (the **offeree**) with the intention that both will be legally bound if it is accepted'.

KEY DEFINITION: Offeror and offeree

An offeror is a person who makes an offer.

An offeree is a person to whom an offer has been made.

EXAM TIP

If you spot what you consider to be an offer in a problem question, explain how it fits within the definition. So if a question begins, 'Giles writes to Fred, asking if Fred wants to buy a second-hand tractor for £3,000 . . .', depending upon the rest of the facts given, this could well be an offer. If you think it is, say so. Define an offer and explain how Giles's letter fits within the definition.

Invitation to treat

It is essential that you can distinguish an offer from an **invitation to treat**.

KEY DEFINITION: Invitation to treat

An invitation to treat is an invitation to bargain, or an invitation to make an offer. The key point is that an invitation to treat is not itself an offer.

If an offer is accepted a contract will result. 'Acceptance' of an invitation to treat cannot create a contract. It might amount to an offer, but that offer would then have to be accepted before a contract would be formed.

KEY CASE

***Pharmaceutical Society of Great Britain* v. *Boots Cash Chemists Ltd* [1953] IQB 401 (CA)**

Concerning: whether goods displayed on supermarket shelves are offers or invitations to treat

Facts

It was a criminal offence to sell certain drugs without a pharmacist being present. The defendants displayed these drugs on the shelves of their supermarket in an area where no pharmacist was present. There was a pharmacist present at the till. The defendants were not guilty.

Legal principle

Goods on supermarket shelves are sold when the contract to sell them is made. The display of such goods is not an offer but only an invitation to treat. The customer makes the offer by taking the goods to the till and offering to pay for them. There the cashier accepts the offer, and sells the goods.

KEY CASE

***Partridge* v. *Crittenden* [1968] 2 All ER 421 (Div Ct)**

Concerning: whether advertisements are usually offers or invitations to treat

Facts

The defendant advertised wild birds for sale. A customer replied and had a bird sent to him. The defendant was charged with the criminal offence of 'offering for sale' a wild bird. The defendant was not guilty. He had not 'offered for sale' the wild bird.

Legal principle

People who advertise goods for sale do not have an unlimited stock of such goods. Therefore, they cannot intend to be making an offer to sell the goods. If the advertisement was an offer, an unlimited number of people could accept. The advertiser would then be in breach of contract for not filling all of the orders.

Because displayed goods are not offers, customers who pick them up and put them in their trolleys have not bought them and can return the goods to the supermarket's shelves.

Offer of a unilateral contract

An offer of a unilateral contract is 'one-sided' because only one person, the offeror, makes a promise. In a bilateral (two-sided) contract both sides exchange promises. In a unilateral contract the offeree does not accept the offer by making a promise, but accepts by performing the act which the offer requested.

KEY CASE

***Carlill* v. *Carbolic Smokeball Co* [1893] 1 QB 256 (CA)**

Concerning: when an advertisement is the offer of a unilateral contract

Facts

The defendants advertised that if anyone used one of their smokeballs properly but still caught flu they would be paid a £100 reward. They also advertised that they had deposited money in a certain bank to show that they meant what they said. The claimant claimed to have done what the advertisement requested but the defendants refused to give her the reward. The defendants had to pay the reward. Their advertisement was the offer of a unilateral contract. The claimant had accepted this offer by performing the acts which the offer had requested.

Legal principle

If the language of an advertisement suggests, to the reasonable person, that the advertisement contains a definite promise to be bound to anyone who performs a requested act it will be the offer of a unilateral contract. Notice that the test is *objective*, depending upon the view of the reasonable person rather than on the views of the parties themselves.

EXAM TIP

Many exam questions consider the distinction between an invitation to treat and an offer of a unilateral contract. To answer such questions apply *Partridge* v. *Crittenden, PSGB* v. *Boots Ltd* and *Carlill*'s case to the problem. If this does not lead to a conclusive answer, follow through both possibilities.

Is the offer still open?

An offer will cease to exist if it is revoked (called off). An offer of a bilateral offer can be revoked at any time unless some consideration (see below) was given for keeping the offer open. An offer will also cease to exist if it is refused by the offeree. A counter offer amounts to a revocation, because it amounts to a refusal of the original offer, whereas a mere request for more information does not.

KEY CASE

***Hyde* v. *Wrench* (1840) 3 Beav 334**

Concerning: the effect of a counter offer

Facts

The defendant offered to sell a farm for £1,000. The claimant replied by saying he would pay £950. This counter offer was refused. The claimant then agreed to pay the £1,000 originally asked. The defendant refused to sell at this price. There was no contract. The counter offer had revoked the original offer.

Legal principle

A counter offer revokes the original offer because it amounts to a refusal of the offer. The offeror is then likely to make a different contract with someone else. It would not make sense to allow the offeree later to insist that the original offer was still open.

A counter offer is not made by a person who merely requests more information about the offer. This request does not amount to a refusal of the offer and so does not revoke it.

KEY CASE

***Stevenson, Jaques & Co* v. *McLean* (1880) 5 QBD 346**

Concerning: distinguishing counter offers and requests for more information

Facts

The defendants offered to sell a quantity of tin to the claimants at a certain price. The offer was to remain open until close of business the following day. The claimants sent a telegram asking if they could pay by instalments. The defendants did not reply. Before the deadline the claimants accepted the offer as originally set out. The defendants were in breach of contract when they refused to deliver the tin.

Legal principle

A mere request for information does not revoke an offer because it is not a refusal of the offer.

EXAM TIP

Many exam questions want you to apply these two cases. If in doubt, go both ways.

At what time is a revocation effective?

A revocation is always effective when it is communicated to (received by) the offeree. The postal rule on acceptance of offers (see below) cannot apply to revocations.

EXAM TIP

Many questions focus on whether or not an offer was still open at the time when it was accepted. Revocation of an offer is effective when it is received by the offeree. So these questions usually come down to analysing who communicated first. Was the offer revoked before it was accepted, in which case there is no contract? Or was it accepted before it was revoked, in which case a contract was formed? But don't forget that acceptance of an offer of a unilateral contract does not need to be communicated. Also the postal rule, considered below, can make a postal acceptance effective when the letter is posted.

Acceptance

A contract will be formed only if an offer which is still open is accepted, without any attempt to vary the terms proposed in the offer. Generally, an acceptance will be effective, and a contract created, when the acceptance is communicated to (received by) the offeror. However, this is not the case if the postal rule (considered below on p. 9) applies or if the acceptance is of a unilateral offer.

Acceptance must be a positive act

Acceptance must be a positive act. It is generally not possible to accept an offer by doing nothing, even if this has been put forward as a method of acceptance. In *Felthouse* v. *Bindley* (1862) an uncle made an offer to his nephew and told him to do nothing if he wanted to accept. The nephew did want to accept and so he did nothing. It was held that there was no contract.

Acceptance of the offer of a unilateral contract

Acceptance of a bilateral offer is effective when it is communicated. When an offer of a unilateral contract is made the offeror has agreed to be bound if some actions are performed. Generally, the performance of these actions will take some time. The offeree begins to accept when he or she begins performance of the requested acts. From this point onwards the offer cannot be revoked. This is the case even if the fact of beginning acceptance has not been communicated to the offeror.

EXAM TIP

Carlill's case can be used as an example. Mrs Carlill began to accept when she first used a smokeball, and finished accepting once she caught flu and claimed the reward. As soon as she had begun to accept, the defendants could not have revoked their offer.

The postal rule

The **postal rule** is an exception to the general rule that an acceptance is effective when it is received.

KEY DEFINITION: Postal rule

The postal rule holds that an acceptance by letter can be effective when it is posted. The rule can apply even to an acceptance which gets lost in the post.

However, you should be aware of the following limitations on the postal rule:

- the rule applies only to an acceptance made by letter or (previously) by telegram;
- the rule will apply only if the letter was properly posted;
- the rule will not apply if to apply it would cause 'manifest inconvenience and absurdity';
- the rule will apply only if an acceptance by post was asked for or reasonably contemplated;
- the rule never applies to revocations, or to anything other than acceptance of an offer;
- the rule will not apply if the offeror stipulated that acceptance would be effective only when it was actually communicated.

KEY CASE

***Holwell Securities Ltd* v. *Hughes* [1974] 1 WLR 155 (CA)**

Concerning: the limits on the postal rule

Facts

An offer was posted. It asked for acceptance 'by notice in writing' within six months. An acceptance was posted but it never arrived. The rule did not apply, because the offer had demanded actual notice of acceptance and so there was no contract. No acceptance had been communicated before the offer expired.

Legal principle

The rule cannot apply if the parties have shown that they do not intend that it should. Nor will the rule apply, Lawton LJ explained, where to apply it would cause 'manifest inconvenience and absurdity'.

REVISION NOTE

An answer which thoughtfully applies *Holwell Securities Ltd* v. *Hughes* is likely to get a good grade.

Offer and acceptance when dealing with machines

Goods are commonly bought from machines. So are tickets which entitle the owner to a service. Obviously, a contract is formed when such tickets are bought. The main reason for wanting to know which side made the offer and which side made the acceptance is that once the contract has been formed it will be too late to introduce new terms into the contract. The same person cannot make both the offer and the acceptance. The general approach is to identify the act which made it impossible not to go through with the contract. This act will be the acceptance. So the other party, the one who did not perform the act which amounted to acceptance, must have made the offer.

Offer and acceptance made over the internet

As yet, no cases have authoritatively dealt with formation of a contract over the internet. So the position can be deduced only by applying common law rules made in cases which did not relate to the internet. Contracts are likely to be made electronically either by an exchange of e-mails or by buying goods displayed on a website.

Exchange of e-mail

The postal rule will not apply. It is restricted to acceptance by letter (or telegram). Analysis of what the parties said in their respective e-mails will enable the court to discover who made the offer and who made the acceptance.

Both revocations and acceptances by e-mail will, following general common law principles, be effective when they are received.

! Don't be tempted to . . .

You should not apply the postal rule to acceptance of an offer by e-mail. There is as yet no precedent on the time at which an e-mail is received, for the purposes of acceptance and revocation. This makes the law in this area uncertain. However, it can be ascertained by applying some cases concerning communication by telex.

In *Entores* v. *Miles Far East Corporation* (1955) the Court of Appeal held that an acceptance by telex is received not when it is sent by the offeree but a second or so later when it is received on the offeror's telex machine. In *Brinkibon Ltd* v. *SSuSmbH* (1983) the House of Lords approved this decision and applied it to a revocation. A telex is a form of near instantaneous communication and is therefore similar to e-mail. The principles set out in *Entores* and *Brinkibon* can be applied to acceptance and revocation by e-mail. In *Brinkibon*, Lord Wilberforce said that disputes about matters such as machines being turned off, or telexes being received out of office hours, could be resolved by reference to the intentions of the parties, by sound business practice and by a judgment as to where the risks should be. This important statement was made in relation to telex messages but should apply equally to an exchange of e-mails.

EXAM TIP

If you answer a question on exchange of e-mails, apply Lord Wilberforce's statement by analogy. First, consider whether the parties showed any intention as to when a message should be effective. Second, consider what sound business practice might be. Third, look for any indications as to where the risks should lie.

Ordering from a website

Generally, goods and services described on a website will be invitations to treat. A website display will be treated like any other advertisement. The customer will usually make an offer by clicking on a button and the website owner will communicate acceptance. The general common law principles on offer and acceptance will apply. However, depending upon what it said, there is no reason why a website should not display the offer of a unilateral contract. If this were to happen then the contract would be formed when the customer performed the requested act. Generally, this would be the act of clicking on a button to indicate acceptance.

Intention to create legal relations

The acceptance of an offer will not create a contract unless the parties intended to enter into a legal relationship. The assessment of whether or not the parties intended to create legal relations will be made objectively, taking account of all of the evidence. So what the parties actually intended is not relevant. The relevant matter is what they appeared, to the reasonable person, to intend.

You should remember the two guiding presumptions: first, that when a social or domestic agreement is made it is presumed that there was no intention to create legal relations; and second, that when an agreement is made in a business or commercial context it is presumed that the parties did intend to make a contract. Either of these presumptions can be overturned by the evidence.

Consideration

You should be able to define consideration and identify it in a problem question. The requirement that consideration should be given by both parties is an essential component of a contract. Apart from this basic idea of consideration, there are several rules relating to consideration. These rules do not follow logically from each other.

What is consideration?

There is no official definition but most people would settle for a definition such as 'a right or benefit to one party or a loss or detriment suffered by another'.

Sufficiency and adequacy

Consideration must be sufficient but need not be adequate. This principle is easily understood if it is realised that sufficient and adequate have special meanings in this context. 'Sufficient' means of some value, 'adequate' means of a value equal to the other party's consideration. So a contract to sell a new car for £1 would be valid.

Figure 1.1

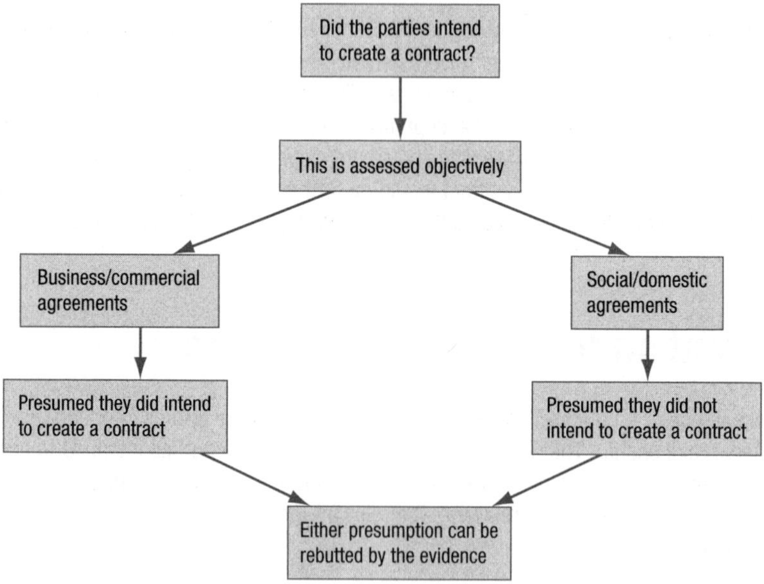

KEY CASE

***Chappell & Co Ltd* v. *Nestlé Co Ltd* [1960] AC 87 (HL)**

Concerning: what can amount to consideration

Facts

The facts of this case are lengthy and complicated and to summarise them here would add little to an understanding of the legal principle outlined below. Remember that examiners are usually looking for an understanding of the *ratio* and legal principle and that reciting the facts in an exam will not improve your grade.

Legal principle

Performing a trivial act which has been requested by the other party can be good consideration. Performance is likely to be a benefit to the person who requested it and a detriment to the person who performs it.

Executed, executory and past consideration

You should know the difference between these three concepts. Executory consideration consists of a promise to do something in the future. Executed consideration occurs when one party makes the offer or acceptance in such a way that he or she completely fulfils his or her obligations under the contract. Both are valid forms of consideration.

Past consideration is no consideration. This rule means that a person cannot give as consideration an act which has already been performed. What appears to be past consideration can be good consideration if it consists of an act which the other party requested and if both sides would all along have contemplated that payment would be made for it.

Promising to perform an existing duty

Whether it is good consideration to promise to perform an existing duty will depend upon how that duty arose.

EXAM TIP

An existing legal duty can have arisen in one of three ways. Many exam questions focus on whether or not a promise to perform an existing duty can amount to good consideration. The technique here is first to identify in which of the three ways the duty arose and then to apply the relevant law.

The duty was imposed by the general law

It is not good consideration to promise to perform a duty which the general law already compels you to perform. It is good consideration to promise to exceed the duty. This area is relatively straightforward.

The duty was imposed under a previous contract with a different person

It is good consideration to promise to perform a duty which has already arisen under a previous contract with a third party. For example, if A has promised B that he will dig B's garden for £100, A can also promise the same act of digging B's garden as consideration in a separate contract under which C promises to pay him £80.

The duty arose under a previous contract with the same person

Historically, it was not good consideration to promise to perform a duty which had already been created under an earlier contract with the promisee. It was good consideration to promise to exceed the duty. The following case must now be considered.

KEY CASE

***Williams* v. *Roffey Bros Ltd* [1990] 2 WLR 1153 (CA)**

Concerning: whether performing an existing duty can be good consideration

Facts

A carpenter agreed with a main contractor that he would do the carpentry work on a block of flats for £20,000. Afterwards the carpenter realised that he had priced the job too low, and said he would not continue. The main contractor needed to finish the block of flats within a certain time or become liable to huge damages. At his own suggestion, the main contractor therefore agreed to pay the carpenter an extra £575 per flat if he agreed to carry on and do what he had previously agreed to do. The carpenter completed work on some more of the flats. The Court of Appeal held that the carpenter had provided extra consideration and that he should be paid the extra amount.

Legal principle

Consideration in this area can be found more easily than in the past. The carpenter's promise to carry on was a benefit to the main contractor because:

- it helped him to avoid paying the huge damages he was worried about;
- it saved him from the trouble of finding another carpenter; and
- it regulated the carpenter's payment in a more organised way than it previously had been.

Part payment of a debt

The common law rule is that a lesser sum of money cannot be consideration for a greater sum owed. This rule was established by the House of Lords in *Foakes* v. *Beer* (1884). There are, however, exceptions to the general rule. In the following cases a debt is extinguished if:

- the creditor agrees to take anything else other than money;
- the creditor asks for and receives early payment of a lesser sum;
- the creditor agrees to take a lesser sum in full payment from a third party;
- the amount owed is disputed and the creditor agrees to take a lesser sum in full settlement of the debt.

Promissory estoppel

The following case might have created another circumstance in which a lesser sum can be good consideration for a greater sum owed.

KEY CASE

***Central London Property Trust Ltd* v. *High Trees House Ltd* [1947] KB 130 (HC) (the High Trees case)**

Concerning: promissory estoppel

Facts

In 1937 the defendants leased a block of flats from the claimants. In 1940 the defendants could not sublet the flats because London was being bombed during the Second World War (1939–45). The claimants agreed to take half rent but did not say for how long. In September 1945, when the war was over, the claimants sued for the whole rent again, but only from the time when the defendants had again been able to fully sublet the flats. Denning J held that the claimants won. He also said that they could not have claimed full rent for the war years because promissory estoppel would have prevented them from doing so.

Legal principle

A promise in return for which no consideration was given might be enforceable if the following conditions are satisfied:

- there must have been an existing legal relationship between the parties;
- the maker of the promise must have intended to create legal relations;
- the promise must have been intended to be acted upon;
- the promise must actually have been acted upon.

You should be aware of the limits of promissory estoppel. If the requirements are found, promissory estoppel might then hold that the promise cannot be broken, even if the promise was to accept a lesser sum of money for a greater sum owed. However:

- it is a shield not a sword, and so can be used only as a defence;
- it is available only to a party who has not behaved inequitably;
- there are uncertainties about the effect of the doctrine, particularly whether it merely suspends obligations until they are reintroduced by reasonable notice or whether it extinguishes rights permanently.

✓ Make your answer stand out

Show that you know Denning J's explanation of promissory estoppel was not the *ratio decidendi* of the case. It was only *obiter dicta* (see p. 181) and therefore not strictly binding. You should be aware of the extent to which other cases support or discredit the idea of promissory estoppel. Answers which can thoughtfully compare these always get good grades.

REVISION NOTE

Remember that a contract will be formed only if there has been an offer, acceptance of that offer and consideration moving both ways. Remember also that the parties must have appeared to intend to create legal relations.

Putting it all together

Answer guidelines

See the problem question at the start of the chapter.

Approaching the question

Obviously, Marc made a contract with Huge Ltd when he bought the camera. You will need to identify whether or not Marc made a second contract with Huge Ltd, under which he has a right to have the price refunded.

Important points to include

- Was the store's price promise the offer of a unilateral contract or just an invitation to treat? Apply *Carlill*'s case to demonstrate that it was the offer of a unilateral contract.
- If the price promise was the offer of a unilateral contract, did Marc perform the act requested? This will depend upon whether or not the postal rule applies.
- Will the postal rule apply? You should explain the rule and apply *Holwell Securities Ltd* v. *Hughes*.

✓ Make your answer stand out

Structure your answer. Explain the requirements of a contract and then use the case law to see if these requirements have been met. Where the law is open to two different interpretations, consider both of them. So if you have doubts as to whether or not the postal rule would apply, follow through both possibilities.

READ TO IMPRESS

Blair, A. (1996) Minding Your Own Business – *Williams* v. *Roffey* Revisited: A Consideration Reconsidered, JBL 254–65

Capps, D. (2004) Electronic Mail and the Postal Rule, 15(7) ICCLR 207–12

Halson, R. (1999) The Offensive Limits of Promissory Estoppel, 2 LMCLQ 256–77

www.pearsoned.co.uk/lawexpress

Go online to access more revision support including quizzes to test your knowledge, sample questions with answer guidelines, podcasts you can download, and more!

Contract 2:
The terms of the contract

2

Revision checklist

Essential points you should know:

- [ ] What constitutes a 'term'
- [ ] The difference between express and implied terms
- [ ] The difference between conditions, warranties and innominate terms
- [ ] The terms implied by the Sale of Goods Act 1979 and by related statutes
- [ ] The extent to which exclusion clauses can exclude or restrict contractual liability
- [ ] How the Consumer Rights Act 2014 will change the law

Topic map

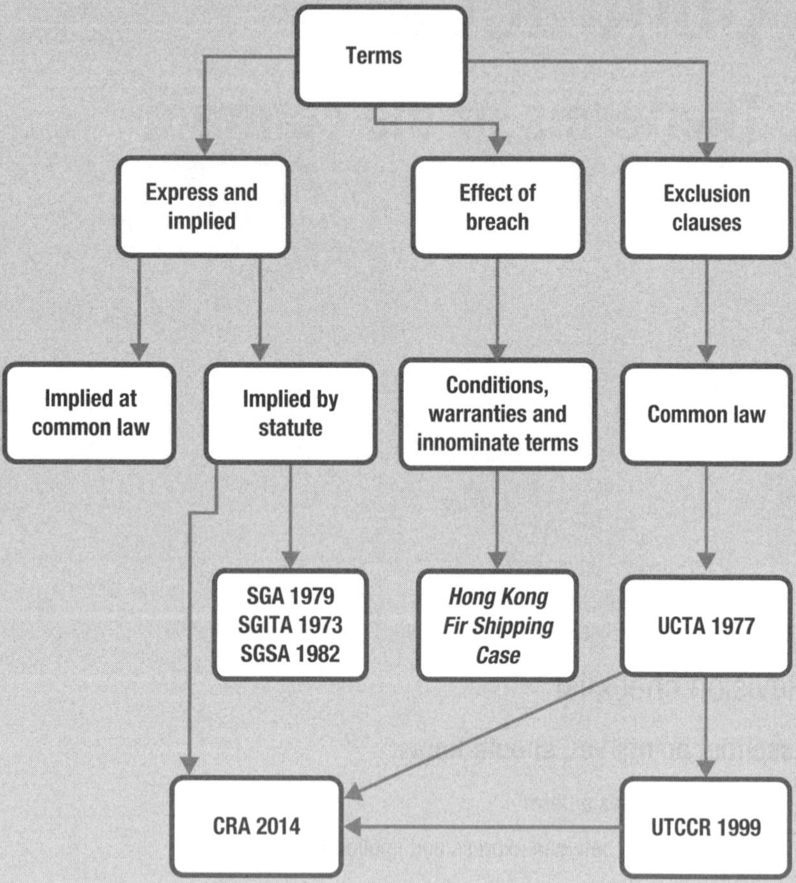

A printable version of this topic map is available from **www.pearsoned.co.uk/lawexpress**

Introduction

Almost any exam question on the law of contract will require a knowledge of the law relating to terms.

The terms of a contract consist of the promises which the parties exchanged when they made the contract. If any of these terms are breached (not performed) the injured party will have a remedy for breach of contract (see Chapter 4). Some terms try to limit or exclude liability for breach of contract. These terms are known as exclusion clauses and their effect is restricted by both the common law and statute.

ASSESSMENT ADVICE

Essay questions

Essay questions on terms tend to focus either on exclusion clauses or on conditions, warranties and innominate terms. So make sure that you can describe the important sections of the Unfair Contract Terms Act 1977 and can explain the differences between the three types of term.

Problem questions

Read the question carefully. Many problem questions are on exclusion clauses. First consider what rights would be available but for the exclusion clause. Then consider whether the clause is a term of the contract and whether the common law invalidates the clause. Then consider the Unfair Contract Terms Act 1977. Finally, if the injured party is a consumer, consider the Unfair Terms in Consumer Contracts Regulations 1999. However, once the Consumer Rights Act 2014 has come into force, and then only if the contract is a consumer contract, apply the CRA 2014 instead of UCTA 1977 and the UTCCR 1999.

Sample question

Could you answer this question? Below is a typical problem question that could arise on this topic. Guidelines on answering the question are included at the end of this chapter, while a sample essay question and guidance on tackling it can be found on the companion website.

PROBLEM QUESTION

Seven weeks ago Jack, who runs a delivery business, bought a two-year-old delivery van for his business from Car Sales Ltd, a local motor dealer. When Jack bought the car he signed a written contract without bothering to read it. This contract said that Car Sales Ltd would have no liability for any defect in the car unless they were notified of the defect within 28 days of purchase. Six weeks after the car was bought its gearbox suddenly seized up. By this time Jack had used the car daily and covered 4,200 miles in it. Expert analysis shows that the defect in the gearbox would have been present when Jack bought the car. Jack contacted Car Sales Ltd to say that he was rejecting the car and wanted a full refund of the price. Car Sales Ltd refused to take the car back or provide any remedy.

Advise Jack of his legal position.

Express and implied terms

Figure 2.1

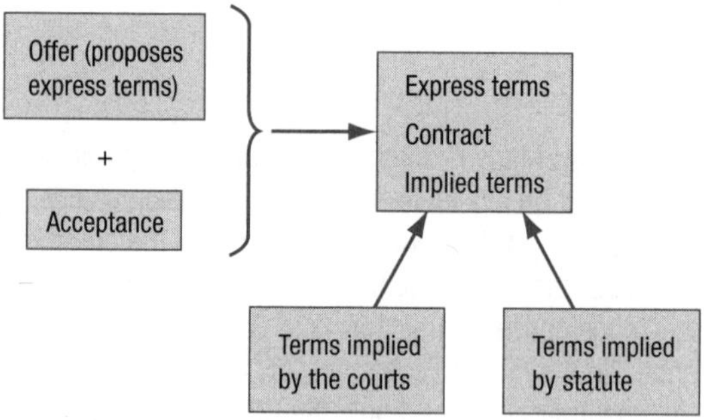

You should know the difference between **express** and **implied terms**.

KEY DEFINITION: Express terms and implied terms

Express terms are expressed by the parties in words. They are contained in the offer which was accepted when the contract was formed.

Implied terms are not expressed by the parties in words.

Terms may be implied either at common law or by statute. The basis on which terms are implied at common law is considered immediately below. The main terms implied by statute are described later in this chapter.

Terms implied at common law

You should know that the common law might imply a term as a matter of fact or as a matter of law. A term is implied as a matter of fact on the grounds that the term was obviously intended by both parties to be a part of the contract. Terms are implied as a matter of law because certain terms are always implied into certain types of contract, such as employment contracts or contracts between landlord and tenant.

REVISION NOTE

The terms implied into contracts of employment are listed in Chapter 9. Terms implied by statute are considered later in this chapter.

Effect of breach of a term

Traditionally all terms were either conditions or warranties. A term which seemed vitally important when the contract was made would be classed as a **condition**, whereas a term which did not seem vitally important would be classed as a **warranty**. If a condition is breached the buyer has two main remedies: to terminate the contract (and possibly to claim damages as well) or merely to claim damages. If a warranty is breached the only remedy available to the buyer is to claim damages.

EXAM TIP

The only reason to distinguish between conditions, warranties and innominate terms is to discover whether or not the buyer is able to terminate the contract. So if a problem question asks you whether a person can terminate a contract you will need to consider what type of term has been breached. If the injured party only wants damages then there is no need to consider what type of term was breached.

In the following, important, case a new type of term, the **innominate (or intermediate) term**, came into being.

KEY CASE

***Hong Kong Fir Shipping Co Ltd* v. *Kawasaki Kisen Kaisha Ltd* [1962] 2 QB 26 (CA)**

Concerning: innominate terms and the remedies available if they are breached

Facts

A ship and its crew were hired out for a two-year period. Various problems with the ship meant that the first five weeks were lost. These problems would take a further

15 weeks to rectify. One of the terms of the contract said that the ship should be 'in every way fitted for ordinary cargo service'. Both sides agreed that this term had been breached. The owners of the ship said it was a mere warranty and that the hirers could not terminate the contract. The hirers said that it was a condition and they were terminating the contract.

Legal principle

A term which covers both major and minor potential breaches cannot be classified in advance as being either a condition or a warranty. It will be an innominate term (a term with no name). If such a term is breached the injured party can always claim damages but can terminate the contract only if 'deprived of substantially the whole benefit' of the contract. In this case the hirers had not been deprived of substantially the whole benefit of the contract and so could not terminate it. This meant that the hirers were themselves in breach of the contract for unjustifiably terminating it.

EXAM TIP

If a term is either a condition or a warranty then it is easy to say whether or not breach allows the injured party to terminate. If the term is an innominate term you must then ask whether the breach which actually occurred deprived the injured party of substantially the whole benefit of the contract. If it did, then the injured party can terminate the contract (and possibly claim damages as well). If it did not, then the injured party cannot terminate the contract but can only claim damages. The key difference is that when considering whether a term is a condition or a warranty, the courts consider how important the term seemed *at the time of the contract.* When considering whether breach of an innominate term allows a party to terminate, the courts consider the seriousness of the breach *which actually happened.*

! Don't be tempted to . . .

You should not think that conditions and warranties no longer exist. Innominate terms have not replaced conditions and warranties altogether. A statute, such as the Sale of Goods Act 1979, might label a term as either a condition or a warranty. Alternatively, the parties might indicate that breach of a particular term will or will not allow the injured party to terminate the contract. If the parties do not do this, and if no statute or other rule of law establishes that the term is a condition or a warranty, then the term is likely to be an innominate term.

Figure 2.2

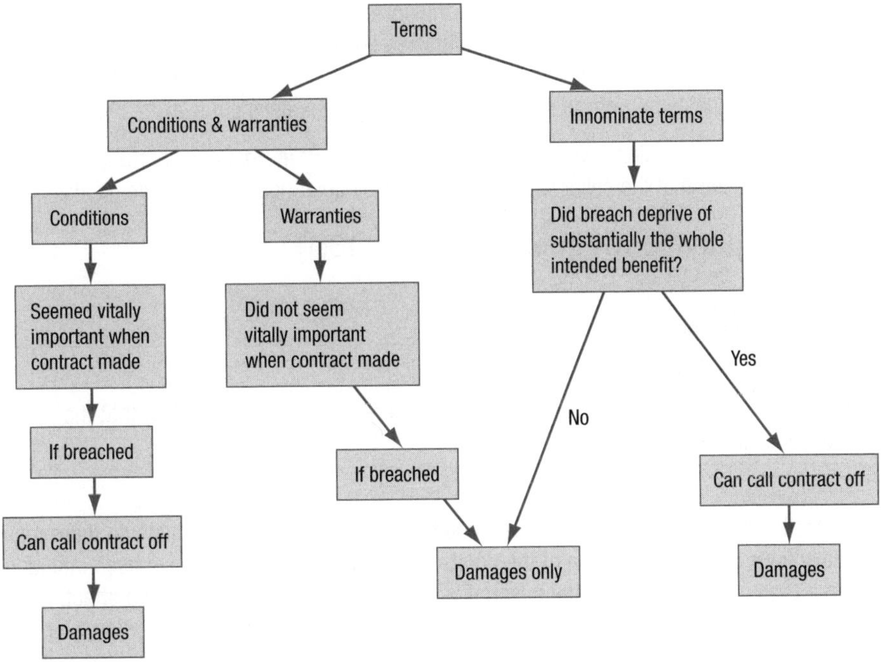

Terms implied by statute

The Sale of Goods Act 1979 implies terms into contracts of sale of goods. Other statutes imply similar terms into other types of contracts. However, you should be aware that when the Consumer Rights Act 2014 comes into force this area of law will be fundamentally changed as regards 'consumer contracts'. The law will be unaltered as regards non-consumer contracts. The CRA 2014, and its definition of a 'consumer contract', is considered later in this chapter (see pp. 37–40).

Sale of Goods Act 1979

The SGA 1979 implies five major terms into all **contracts of sale of goods**.

KEY DEFINITION: Contract of sale of goods

A contract is a sale of goods only if a buyer pays money, or promises to pay money, in return for the ownership of goods. Goods are physical things which can be touched and moved. Services are not goods, nor are land or houses.

The right to sell: s. 12(1)

There is an implied condition on the part of the seller that he or she has the right to sell the goods. This is the most fundamental of the implied terms because a seller who does not have the right to sell will not have the right to transfer ownership to the buyer. Generally, a seller will not have the right to sell goods which he or she does not own.

Section 12(2) implies minor warranties that the goods are free from any charge or encumbrance and that the seller will continue to enjoy quiet possession of the goods.

Correspondence with description: s. 13(1)

KEY STATUTE

Sale of Goods Act 1979, s. 13(1)

Where there is a sale of goods by description, there is an implied condition that the goods will correspond with the description.

This section is surprisingly complex. The goods must be sold 'by description', so there must actually have been a description of the goods and the description must have been intended to be a term of the contract. If the description was a 'mere puff' it will have no effect. If it was a representation, there might or might not be a remedy for misrepresentation (see Chapter 3).

EXAM TIP

Section 13(1) will not apply unless the description was a term of the contract. So the only reason for a buyer to argue that s. 13 does apply is that s. 13 makes the term a *condition*. If a descriptive term is not within s. 13(1) it might be a warranty or an innominate term. (The different consequences of breach of condition, warranty and innominate term were considered earlier in this chapter.)

KEY STATUTE

Sale of Goods Act 1979, s. 14(2)

Where the seller sells goods in the course of a business, there is an implied condition that the goods supplied under the contract are of satisfactory quality.

Satisfactory quality: s. 14(2)

Section 14(2) requires the goods 'supplied under the contract' to be of satisfactory quality. It therefore extends to packaging, to 'buy one, get one free' and even to returnable goods in which the goods actually sold are delivered.

EXAM TIP

Many questions are asked on s. 14(2). The correct approach is as follows. First consider the circumstances in which s. 14(2) will apply. Then consider the definition in s. 14(2A). Then, if relevant, consider the aspects of quality set out in s. 14(2B). Finally, if the term is breached, consider the remedies available.

Circumstances in which s. 14(2) will not apply

Section 14(2) will apply only if the goods were sold 'in the course of a business'. In *Stevenson* v. *Rogers* (1999), the Court of Appeal held that whenever a business sells anything it does so in the course of a business, for the purposes of s. 14 of the SGA.

Section 14(2C) provides two further limitations. First, the implied term will not extend to defects which were specifically drawn to the buyer's attention before the contract was made. Second, where the buyer examined the goods before the contract was made, the term will not apply as regards defects which that examination ought to have revealed. Remember, though, that the buyer has no obligation to examine the goods and that the more thorough the examination made the less the buyer will be protected.

Meaning of satisfactory quality

The requirement of satisfactory quality was introduced in 1995, replacing a requirement of merchantable quality. Section 14(2A) gives the definition of satisfactory quality and (2B) lists five aspects of quality in appropriate cases.

KEY STATUTE

Sale of Goods Act 1979, s. 14(2A) and (2B)

(2A) Goods are of satisfactory quality if they meet the standard that a reasonable person would regard as satisfactory, taking account of any description of the goods, the price (if relevant) and all the other relevant circumstances.

(2B) The quality of goods includes their state and condition and the following (among others) are in appropriate cases aspects of the quality of the goods –

(a) fitness for all the purposes for which goods of the kind in question are commonly supplied,

(b) appearance and finish,

(c) freedom from minor defects,

(d) safety, and

(e) durability.

Do not forget that the definition of satisfactory quality is contained in s. 14(2A). The five factors listed in s. 14(2B) are only aspects of quality *in appropriate cases*. In some cases, such as when new consumer goods are bought, all of the aspects of quality are likely to be appropriate. But in other cases, such as when a car is sold for scrap, none of the aspects of quality listed in s. 14(2B) would be relevant because it would not be appropriate to consider any of the aspects of quality.

KEY CASE

***Bramhill* v. *Edwards* [2004] EWCA Civ 403 (CA)**

Concerning: the test of satisfactory quality

Facts

The facts of this case are lengthy and complicated and to summarise them here would add little to an understanding of the legal principle outlined below.

Legal principle

The Court of Appeal made it plain that the test of satisfactory quality is an *objective* test. It focuses on the opinion of the reasonable person in the position of the buyer, with the buyer's background knowledge.

Fitness for purpose: s. 14(3)

Where goods are sold in the course of a business and the buyer expressly or impliedly makes known to the seller any particular purpose for which the goods are being bought, then there is an implied condition that the goods are reasonably fit for that purpose. This is the case even if the purpose made known is not a purpose for which such goods are commonly supplied.

Section 14(3) will not apply if:

- the seller did not sell the goods in the course of a business (*Stevenson* v. *Rogers* will again provide the test);
- the buyer does not rely on the skill and judgement of the seller;
- it is unreasonable for the buyer to rely on the skill and judgement of the seller.

Where goods are bought and used for their ordinary purpose s. 14(3) will apply. The buyer will be taken to have made the purpose known to the seller and to have relied on the skill and judgement of the seller.

Sale by sample: s. 15(2)

Where goods are sold by sample s. 15(2) implies two conditions:

- that the bulk of the goods will correspond with the sample in quality; and
- that the goods will be free from any defects, making their quality unsatisfactory, if these defects would not be apparent on reasonable examination of the sample.

✓ Make your answer stand out

Notice that the approach taken by s. 15(2) differs from the approach taken by s. 14(2). Section 14(2) does not require the buyer to examine the goods. A buyer who does examine the goods can lose protection because s. 14(2) will then not protect as regards defects which that examination ought to have revealed. Section 15(2) does expect the buyer to examine the sample. If both the sample and the bulk contain defects which would render the goods unsatisfactory, and these defects would be apparent on a reasonable examination of the sample, a buyer who fails to notice the defects in the sample will have no remedy under s. 14(2) or under s. 15(2).

Supply of Goods Implied Terms Act 1973

The SGITA 1973 implies terms which are identical to those implied by the SGA 1979 into contracts of hire-purchase. A contract of hire-purchase is one under which a person hires goods for a fixed period and is given an option to purchase those goods for a nominal sum at the end of the period.

Supply of Goods and Services Act 1982, Part 1

The SGSA 1982, Part 1 implies terms which are identical to those implied by the SGA 1979 into two different types of contract: first, into contracts for the transfer of property in goods; second, into contracts of hire.

A contract for the transfer of property in goods is one under which ownership of goods is transferred, where the contract is not a sale of goods nor a contract of hire-purchase. It could be a contract of barter, where goods are simply exchanged. Or it could be a contract to supply a service where the contract incidentally involves the ownership of some goods being transferred. So, for example, a contract to repair a central heating boiler would be a contract to provide a service. But if this involved some minor parts being replaced then, as regards these spare parts, it would also be a contract for the transfer of property in goods.

Figure 2.3 shows which section of which statute implies the relevant term.

Figure 2.3

Type of contract / Term implied	**Sale of goods** (SGA 1979)	**Hire-purchase** (SGITA 1973)	**Transfer of property in goods** (SGSA 1982)	**Hire** (SGSA 1982)
Right to sell	s. 12(1)	s. 8	s. 2	s. 7
Quiet possession & freedom from encumbrances	s. 12(2)	s. 8	s. 2	s. 7
Correspondence with description	s. 13	s. 9	s. 3	s. 8
Satisfactory quality in business sales	s. 14(2)	s. 10(2)	s. 4(2)	s. 9(2)
Fitness for purpose in business sales	s. 14(3)	s. 10(3)	s. 4(3)	s. 9(3)
Correspondence with sample	s. 15	s. 11	s. 5	s. 10

Supply of Goods and Services Act 1982, Part 2

The SGSA 1982, Part 2 implies three terms into contracts for the supply of a service. These terms have no equivalent in the SGA 1979. They are as follows:

- Section 13(1) – implies a term that a supplier providing a service in the course of a business will carry out the service with reasonable care and skill.
- Section 14(1) – implies a term that a service provided by a supplier acting in the course of a business will be carried out within a reasonable time (where the contract did not fix a time by which the service should be carried out).
- Section 15(1) – implies a term that the price for the supply of a service will be a reasonable price (where the contract did not fix a price).

Section 13(1) of the SGSA 1982 imposes a tort standard, a standard of reasonable care and skill. It is quite different from s. 14(2) and (3) SGA 1979, both of which impose **strict liability**, that is to say liability without fault. So s. 14(2) of the SGA 1979 can be breached even where a seller is not in any way at fault and has no idea that the goods supplied are not of satisfactory quality (for example, where a shop sells heavily packaged goods which turn out to be faulty). Section 13(1) of the SGSA 1982 will never make a provider of a service liable unless he or she failed to carry out a service with reasonable care and skill.

REVISION NOTE

The standard of care demanded by the tort of negligence is considered in Chapter 5. Remember that this is the standard required by s. 13(1) of the SGSA 1982. Remember also that if there is a contract to supply a service and some goods are incidentally transferred under the contract, then s. 13(1) of the SGSA 1982 will apply to the service element of the contract and ss. 2–5 of the SGSA 1982 will apply to the transfer of property element of the contract.

The status of the statutory implied terms

All of the terms in the SGA 1979 are labelled as conditions or warranties. If the condition in s. 12(1) is breached the buyer can always terminate the contract and get a full refund of the price. If the warranty in s. 12(2) is breached the buyer cannot terminate the contract but can claim damages.

Sections 13–15 of the SGA 1979 are classified as conditions. So if these terms are breached the starting point is that the buyer can terminate the contract and claim a refund of the price. However, the SGA 1979, s. 15A requires a buyer who does not deal as a consumer to treat a breach of ss. 13–15 as a breach of warranty if the breach is so slight as to make it unreasonable to reject the goods. Furthermore, s. 11(4) provides that a buyer who has 'accepted' the goods will only be able to treat a breach of ss. 13–15 as a breach of warranty. The complex definition of 'dealing as a consumer' is considered later (see p. 35).

Section 35 provides that a buyer can be deemed to have accepted goods in three ways:

- by keeping them for more than a reasonable time without rejecting them;
- by intimating acceptance of them; or
- by doing an act which is inconsistent with the seller's continuing ownership. (Essentially, this means doing something to the goods which would prevent them from being returned to the seller in much the same condition as they were when they were bought.)

Both SGITA 1973 and SGSA 1982, Part 1 contain an equivalent of s. 15A of the SGA 1979. But neither statute contains an equivalent of s. 11(4) or s. 35 of the SGA 1979.

Figure 2.4 shows the circumstances in which a breach of one of the SGA 1979 statutory implied terms, or of the equivalent terms in the SGITA 1973 or the SGSA 1982, Part 1, will allow a buyer to terminate the contract.

Figure 2.4

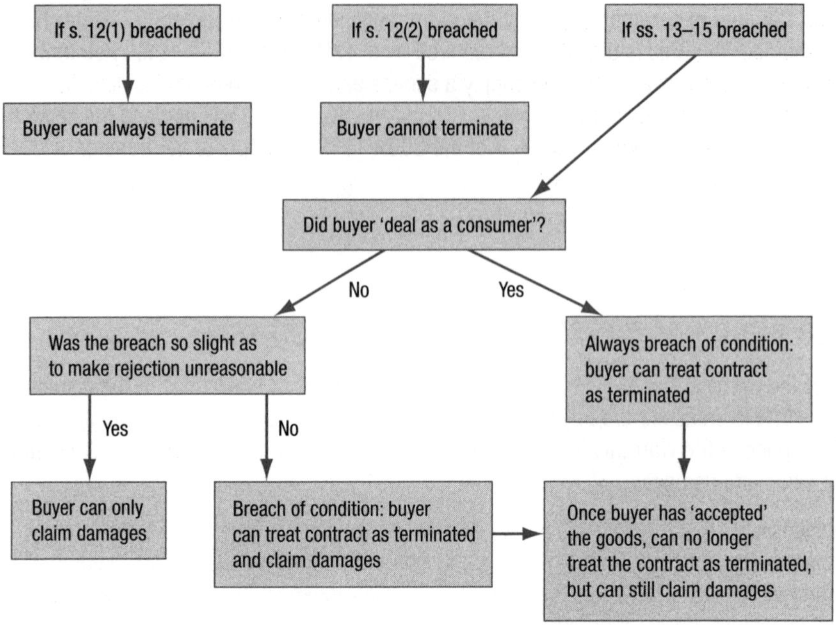

The term implied by s. 13(1) of the SGSA 1982 is an innominate term (see p. 23).

EXAM TIP

Approach problem questions about the right to terminate for breach of a statutory implied term in this order. First, classify the transaction as a sale of goods, a contract of hire-purchase, a contract of hire, a contract to transfer property in goods or a contract to provide a service. (Remember that a contract can be both a contract to transfer property in goods and a contract to provide a service.) Second, use Figure 2.3 to see which section of which statute implies the term which has been breached. Third, use Figure 2.4 to see if the customer can terminate the contract.

Additional remedies of the buyer in consumer cases

Part 5A of the SGA 1979 gives additional remedies to a buyer who deals as a consumer if the goods do not conform to the contract at the time of delivery. For the complex definition of dealing as a consumer, see below in relation to exclusion clauses (on p. 33). Goods do not conform to the contract if an **express term** of the contract is breached, or if one of the terms contained in ss. 13–15 of the SGA is breached. If goods do not conform to the contract within six months of the date of delivery it is presumed that they did not conform to the contract at the date of delivery. The burden will therefore be on the seller to show that they did conform.

The hierarchy of rights

If the two requirements of Part 5A are satisfied the buyer may choose between the first two remedies in the hierarchy. These remedies are either repair or replacement of the goods. Then the seller must perform the remedy within a reasonable time and at his or her own expense. But a buyer cannot insist upon a remedy which is impossible or which is disproportionate, compared with another remedy. A remedy is disproportionate if it would impose unreasonable costs upon the seller.

The secondary remedies are reducing the contract price by an appropriate amount and rescission of the contract. These remedies cannot be claimed as of right. They can be claimed only if:

- repair or replacement is impossible; or
- repair or replacement is disproportionate in relation to one of the secondary remedies; or
- the buyer has required the seller to repair or replace the goods but the seller has not done so within a reasonable time and without significant inconvenience to the buyer.

If the contract is rescinded under Part 5A the court has the power to reduce the amount of the price which is refunded so as to take account of any use of the goods which the buyer has had. The court also has the power to adjust any of the new remedies as it sees fit and so could also award damages.

These additional rights are also available when ss. 3–5 SGSA 1982 are breached.

Exclusion clauses

Exclusion clauses try to exclude or restrict liability for breach of contract.

EXAM TIP

A problem question on exclusion clauses should be answered in a certain way. First, consider whether the clause was incorporated into the contract. Next, identify the breach of contract which occurred, and whether the wording of the clause excludes liability for such a breach. Next, consider the effect of the Unfair Contract Terms Act 1977. Finally, if relevant, consider the effect of the Unfair Terms in Consumer Contracts Regulations 1999. However, once the Consumer Rights Act 2014 is in force you will need to apply this Act, instead of UCTA 1977 and the 1999 Regs, if the contract is a consumer contract. If the contract is a non-consumer contract you will apply UCTA 1977. The 1999 Regs will be repealed once the CRA 2014 is in force.

Is the exclusion clause incorporated into the contract?

The common law has made various rules as follows:

- a person who signs a document will generally be bound by its contents, whether the document has been read or not;
- a person who misrepresents the effect of an exclusion clause may not be able to rely on it.
- a clause contained in a document which the reasonable person would think was part of the contract will be incorporated;
- a clause will be incorporated if the other party was given reasonable notice of the clause before the contract was made;
- a clause can become incorporated into the contract because of a course of dealing between the parties, or because it is customary in a certain trade.

Does the wording cover the breach?

This is just a matter of construction of contractual terms. However, the *contra proferentum* rule says that any ambiguity will be resolved against the wishes of the party trying to rely on the clause.

Unfair Contract Terms Act 1977

UCTA 1977 applies only to business liability. Once the Consumer Rights Act 2014 is in force it will cease to apply to consumer contracts but will continue to apply to non-consumer contracts.

KEY STATUTE

Unfair Contract Terms Act 1977, s. 2(1), (2) and 3

Section 2(1) provides that no contract term can exclude liability for death or personal injury resulting from negligence. Negligence is defined by s. 1 as including failing to take reasonable care in the performance of a contractual obligation.

Section 2(2) provides that liability for other types of loss or damage resulting from negligence can be excluded if the term excluding liability satisfies the UCTA requirement of reasonableness.

Section 3 provides that an exclusion clause cannot protect a party against liability for breach of contract unless it satisfies the requirement of reasonableness, and cannot protect a party who fails to perform the contract at all, or who performs in a manner different from what was reasonably expected, unless it satisfies the requirement of reasonableness. However, s. 3 protects only those who *deal as a consumer* or *who deal on the other party's written standard terms.*

Meaning of dealing as a consumer

Several sections of UCTA 1977 and SGA 1979 protect buyers only if they deal as a consumer. The definition of dealing as a consumer, for both UCTA 1977 and SGA 1979, is contained in s. 12 UCTA 1977. A buyer deals as a consumer if:

1. he neither makes the contract in the course of a business, nor holds himself out as doing so; and
2. the other party does make the contract in the course of a business; and
3. the goods supplied under the contract are of a type ordinarily supplied for private use or consumption. (Notice that this final requirement applies only if the buyer is a company.)

Even a business can deal as a consumer when buying goods. In *R&B Customs Brokers Ltd* v. *United Dominions Trust Ltd* (1988) the Court of Appeal held that a business buys goods 'in the course of a business' in only three circumstances:

- if the goods were the type of goods which the business was in business to buy and sell;
- if the goods were bought to be sold at a profit;
- if the company had previously bought the same type of goods fairly regularly.

So, in *R& B Customs Brokers*, an import and export company which bought a car did not buy it in the course of a business because it had not bought cars frequently before, and it did not buy the car to sell it at a profit.

! Don't be tempted to . . .

You should not think that the words 'in the course of a business' have one fixed meaning in the SGA 1979. The words are given one meaning when considering whether or not a person deals as a consumer, in both UCTA 1977 and SGA 1979. They are given a quite different meaning by *Stevenson* v. *Rogers* when considering whether or not goods were sold 'in the course of a business' for the purposes of s. 14 of the SGA. This is unfortunate. However, you should be aware of both definitions and the circumstances in which they are used. Once the Consumer Rights Act 2014 is in force the whole concept of 'dealing as a consumer' will cease to exist. The CRA 2014 (considered on pp. 37–40) will apply to 'consumer contracts'. UCTA 1977 will apply to non-consumer contracts.

KEY STATUTE

Unfair Contract Terms Act 1977, ss. 6–8

Sections 6 and 7 of UCTA 1977 deal with exclusion of the statutory implied terms contained in the SGA 1979, and with the equivalent terms in the SGITA 1973 and the SGSA 1982. Sections 6 and 7 make a distinction between those who deal as a ▶

consumer and those who do not. As regards a buyer who *deals as a consumer*, the statutory implied terms contained in ss. 13–15 of the SGA 1979, and their equivalents in the SGITA 1973 and the SGSA 1982, can never be excluded. As regards a buyer who does not deal as a consumer these terms can be excluded, but only by a term which satisfies the UCTA *requirement of reasonableness*. The term contained in s. 12(1) of the SGA, and its equivalent in the SGITA 1973 and the SGSA 1982, can never be excluded. Section 8 of UCTA 1977 provides that no term can restrict liability for misrepresentation, unless the term satisfies the requirement of reasonableness.

The requirement of reasonableness

Section 11 of UCTA provides that the requirement of reasonableness is satisfied if the term shall have been a fair and reasonable one to be included having regard to the circumstances which were, or ought reasonably to have been, known to or in the contemplation of the parties when the contract was made.

Schedule 2 to UCTA lists five other matters to which regard must be paid:

1. the relative strength of the bargaining positions of the parties;
2. whether the customer was given any inducement to agree to the exclusion clause or could have made the contract elsewhere without agreeing to a similar term;
3. whether the customer knew or ought to have known of the term's existence and extent;
4. if the term excludes or restricts liability unless some condition is complied with, whether or not it was reasonably practicable to comply with that condition;
5. whether the goods were manufactured, altered or adapted at the customer's request.

Unfair Terms in Consumer Contracts Regulations 1999

These Regulations apply alongside UCTA 1977, they do not replace it. They will be replaced by the Consumer Rights Act 2014 when it comes into force. The Regulations apply only to contracts made between a '**seller or supplier**' and a 'consumer'.

KEY DEFINITION: Seller or supplier

A 'seller or supplier' is defined by the UTCC Regs as a person who is acting for purposes relating to his trade, business or profession.

! Don't be tempted to . . .

You should not think that the UTCC Regs have adopted the UCTA 1977 definition of 'dealing as a consumer'. The definition of a consumer in the UTCC Regs is quite different from the definition of 'dealing as a consumer' in UCTA 1977 and the SGA 1979. The Regulations define a consumer as a natural person (and so never a company) who is acting for purposes outside his trade, business or profession. We have already considered the complex definition of dealing as a consumer for the purposes of the SGA 1979 and UCTA 1977. You must use the appropriate definition when applying UCTA, the SGA or the UTCC Regs.

Regulation 5 provides that a contractual term which has not been individually negotiated shall be regarded as unfair if, contrary to the requirement of good faith, it causes a significant imbalance in the parties' rights and obligations arising under the contract, to the detriment of the consumer. If the term is regarded as unfair, reg. 8 provides that it is not binding upon the consumer although the rest of the contract will stand if this is possible without the unfair term.

The Regulations will not invalidate a 'core term' which was written in plain and intelligible language. A core term sets out the contract price and the main subject matter of the contract.

Schedule 2 to the Regulations sets out a long list of examples of terms which may be regarded as unfair.

The Consumer Rights Act 2014

When the CRA 2014 comes into force the law relating to the statutory implied terms and exclusion clauses will be changed as regards **consumer contracts**. The law will not be changed as regards non-consumer contracts.

KEY DEFINITIONS: Consumer/trader/consumer contract

Section 1 CRA 2014 provides that the Act applies to consumer contracts, which means contracts where a trader supplies or agrees to supply goods, digital content (software) or services to a consumer. Section 2 defines both 'trader' and 'consumer'. A trader is defined as a person acting (personally or through an agent) for purposes relating to his trade, business, craft or profession. A consumer is defined as an individual acting for purposes that are mainly or wholly outside that individual's trade, business, craft or profession. Because a consumer must be an individual, a company or LLP cannot be a consumer.

The CRA implied terms relating to goods

If a contract is a consumer contract to acquire goods, the CRA implies terms as to:

- the right to sell;
- correspondence with description and sample;
- satisfactory quality; and
- fitness for purpose.

These terms are identical to the SGA 1979 implied terms. There is also an additional term that goods will correspond with any model by which they were sold. If any of these terms are breached the goods will be regarded as not conforming to the contract.

! Don't be tempted to . . .

You should not be tempted to think that it is still necessary to use different statutes, depending upon whether the contract was one of sale, hire, hire-purchase, barter or installation. If the contract is a consumer contract to acquire goods or digital content (software) then the contract will be governed by the CRA 2014.

Remedies if goods fail to conform

The implied terms are no longer regarded as conditions, warranties or innominate terms. Instead, five remedies might be available if the goods do not conform to the contract. These remedies are:

- **the early right to reject**;
- **repair** or **replacement**; and (possibly)
- **price reduction** or the **final right to reject**.

The early right to reject entitles the consumer to a full refund of the price and is therefore similar to rejecting for breach of condition. It can be lost in two ways; by failing to reject within the time limit for rejecting the goods or by accepting the goods. The time limit is 30 days after delivery of the goods unless the goods are perishable. Acceptance does not have the same meaning as it does under the SGA 1979. Under the CRA 2014 a consumer accepts goods only if he indicates to the trader that he accepts the goods, after having had a reasonable opportunity to examine the goods to find out if they conform to the contract. If the early right to reject is lost, or if he or she chooses to do so, a consumer can choose between repair or replacement of non-conforming goods. The rules which apply here are the same as those which would previously have applied to Part 5A SGA (as set out above on pp. 32 and 33). The secondary remedies of price reduction and the final right to reject (called rescission in Part 5A) are available in the same circumstances as they were under Part 5A.

The CRA implied terms relating to services

The CRA 2014 implies a term that any service provided under a consumer contract must be provided using reasonable care and skill. Furthermore, any information provided by the trader is to be treated as an express term of the contract if it was taken into account by the consumer when deciding to enter into the contract. If these terms are breached the consumer can require repeat performance of the contract. But if this is not possible, or has been requested by the consumer but not performed by the trader within a reasonable time, and without causing significant inconvenience to the consumer, the consumer can have a price reduction.

The CRA as it applies to exclusion clauses

If a contract is a non-consumer contract then it will be governed by UCTA 1977, rather than by the CRA 2014. The CRA 2014 has no effect on UCTA 1977 except in relation to consumer contracts and consumer notices. However, the CRA 2014 repeals and replaces the Unfair Terms in Consumer Contracts Regulations 1999. A consumer contract for the purposes of the CRA 2014, was defined above (on p. 37). A consumer notice is a notice or announcement which relates to rights and obligations between a trader and a consumer or which purports to exclude or restrict a trader's liability to a consumer. Neither an **unfair consumer term** nor an **unfair consumer notice** is binding upon a consumer.

KEY DEFINITION: Unfair consumer term or notice

A consumer term or notice is unfair if, contrary to the requirement of good faith, it causes a significant imbalance in the parties' rights and obligations to the detriment of the consumer.

Whether or not a term is fair is to be determined (a) taking into account the nature of the subject matter of the contract, and (b) by reference to all of the surrounding circumstances, including the other terms of the contract. However, 'core terms', which relate to the main subject matter of the contract or the appropriateness of the price cannot be assessed for unfairness.

A trader must ensure that a written term of a consumer contract or consumer notice is transparent. Any particularly onerous or unusual term must be drawn particularly to the consumer's attention. A 'grey list' sets out 20 indicative and non-exhaustive list of terms which may be regarded as unfair.

Effect of a term or notice being unfair

Neither an unfair contract term nor an unfair contract notice is binding upon a consumer. Where a contract term or notice is not binding on a consumer on account of being unfair the contract continues, as far as practicable, to have effect in every other respect.

Exclusion of liability

A trader cannot, by either a consumer contract or a consumer notice, exclude or restrict liability for death or personal injury resulting from negligence. This is similar to the rule set out in s. 2(1) UCTA 1977.

If a trader tries to exclude liability of loss other than death or personal injury caused by negligence the term or notice which excludes liability will be invalid if it is an unfair term or notice.

Liability for breach of any of the CRA 2014 implied terms relating to goods, digital content or services cannot be excluded or restricted by any term of a consumer contract or by any consumer notice.

✓ Make your answer stand out

Question whether it makes sense to have a definition of a consumer in the UTCC Regs which is so different from the concept of 'dealing as a consumer' in UCTA 1977 and the SGA 1979. Which definition provides the wider scope for consumer protection? Is the position of consumers improved by the Consumer Rights Act 2014?

Putting it all together

Answer guidelines

See the problem question at the start of the chapter.

Approaching the question

Jack has made a contract with the shop. He can reject the car and claim a full refund if a condition has been breached and if the exclusion clause in the contract is ineffective.

Important points to include

You will need to consider the following:

- Have any of the SGA 1979 implied terms been breached? If so, is the term a condition? You should concentrate on ss. 14(2) and 14(3).

- Will either s. 11(4) or s. 15A prevent Jack from rejecting? If he is prevented from rejecting, what remedy will Jack have?
- Did Jack 'deal as a consumer'? If he did, what additional remedies might be available to him under Part 5A SGA. Are these remedies any better than the remedies which Jack already has?
- Was the exclusion clause incorporated into the contract, even if Jack did not read it? It would seem that it was, so you must explain this.
- Would the wording of the clause allow Car Sales Ltd to refuse a refund? Again, this seems to be the case.
- Would UCTA 1977 invalidate the exclusion clause? You will need to consider whether or not Jack dealt as a consumer and then apply ss. 6 and 7 UCTA. If in doubt as to whether or not Jack dealt as a consumer you must consider both possibilities.
- You should explain why the UTCC Regs 1999 would not apply because they would not regard Jack as being a consumer, even if the SGA 1979 might regard him as having 'dealt as a consumer'.
- Finally, if the Consumer Rights Act 2014 is in force you should explain why it will not apply as the contract which Jack made would not have been a 'consumer contract'.

✓ Make your answer stand out

Plan your answer logically. First deal with whether any terms have been breached. Then go on to consider whether the breached terms were conditions, warranties or innominate terms. If relevant, consider acceptance and the additional rights in consumer cases. If the question concerns an exclusion clause, consider the common law, then UCTA 1977 and then, if relevant, the UTCC Regs 1999. Show that you understand concepts such as being a consumer (for the purposes of the UTCC Regs 1999) and dealing as a consumer (for the purposes of UCTA 1977 and the SGA 1979).

READ TO IMPRESS

Ervine, W. (2004) Satisfactory Quality: What Does It Mean? JBL 684–703

Hashemi, A. (2001) Exclusion Clauses in Business Contracts, 12(3) *Practical Law Companies* 16–18

Twigg-Flesner, C. (2004) The Relationship between Satisfactory Quality and Fitness for Purpose, 63(1) CLJ 22–4

www.pearsoned.co.uk/lawexpress

Go online to access more revision support including quizzes to test your knowledge, sample questions with answer guidelines, podcasts you can download, and more!

Contract 3:

Misrepresentation, mistake, duress, illegality, minors and privity

Revision checklist

Essential points you should know:

- [ ] The definition of an actionable misrepresentation and the remedies available
- [ ] The different types of mistake which can make a contract void
- [ ] The difference between duress and undue influence
- [ ] The types of contracts which are illegal or void at common law
- [ ] The legal effect of contracts made by minors
- [ ] The meaning of privity of contract and the effect of the Contracts (Rights of Third Parties) Act 1999

Topic map

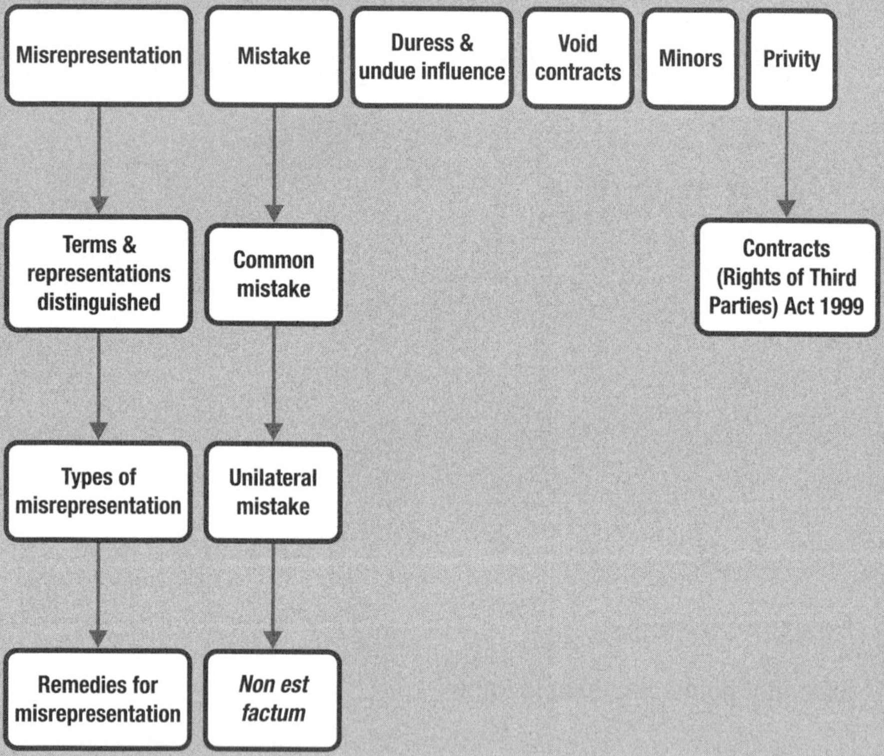

A printable version of this topic map is available from **www.pearsoned.co.uk/lawexpress**

Introduction

This chapter considers five commonly examined matters that can make a contract either void, voidable or unenforceable.

Misrepresentation is the most important of these factors. The distinction between void contracts and voidable contracts is very significant. A void contract confers no legal rights on anyone. A voidable contract is valid but one party has the option to avoid it (make it void) within a reasonable time.

ASSESSMENT ADVICE

First you must decide which of the five matters dealt with by this chapter the question relates to. Questions may be about two or more of the matters. This is particularly the case with questions about buying goods from a rogue. Such questions usually concern both mistake and misrepresentation.

Make sure that a question which seems to be about misrepresentation is not about terms (considered in Chapter 2). If an untrue statement is a representation, then the question is likely to be about whether or not there has been a misrepresentation. If an untrue statement is a term, the question is likely to be about whether or not there has been breach of contract and, if so, whether the injured party can call off the contract. If relevant, make sure that you clearly explain the different consequences of a contract being void or voidable.

Sample question

Could you answer this question? Below is a typical problem question that could arise on this topic. Guidelines on answering the question are included at the end of this chapter, while a sample essay question and guidance on tackling it can be found on the companion website.

PROBLEM QUESTION

On Monday a man who claimed to be Professor Smith of Nottville University persuaded Jacek to take a cheque for his car. On Wednesday Jacek's bank told him that the cheque had been stolen and that the man who had given it to Jacek was a rogue pretending to be Professor Smith. Jacek immediately asked the police to look out for the car. On Tuesday the rogue had sold the car to Nisha, who bought it in good faith.

Advise Jacek of his legal position.

Misrepresentation

The difference between terms and representations

If a term is breached, there will always be a remedy for breach of contract. If a representation is untrue there might be a claim for misrepresentation. An action for misrepresentation is quite different from an action for breach of contract. So first it is important to distinguish terms and representations.

> **EXAM TIP**
>
> When a contract is written, the general rule is that the terms of the contract will be contained in the written document. Statements which are not included in the written document will be representations.

An oral statement made before a contract is completed might be either a term or a representation. Which it is will depend upon the objectively assessed intentions of the parties. The following tests have been used to tell whether the parties intended a statement to be a term or a representation. However, it is important to remember that these tests are not decisive. All of the evidence will be assessed to discover the true intentions of the parties.

- Strong statements are likely to be terms, weak statements are likely to be representations.
- If a party demonstrated that a statement was considered to be vitally important, then that statement is likely to be a term.
- The party with the greater knowledge or skill is likely to make terms. The party with the lesser knowledge or skill is likely to make representations.

Section 1(a) of the Misrepresentation Act 1967 allows for the possibility of a misrepresentation later becoming a term. For example, a statement made during negotiations could later be put into a written contract. If this happens, remedies for both misrepresentation and breach of contract may become available.

Some statements are so vague, or so obviously a mere opinion, that they are neither terms nor representations. Traditionally such statements, which have no legal effect, have been called 'mere puffs'.

> **EXAM TIP**
>
> In an exam question make sure you know whether a statement is a term, a representation or a mere puff. If in doubt, consider all possibilities.

Actionable misrepresentations

KEY DEFINITION: Actionable misrepresentation

An actionable misrepresentation is an untrue statement of fact which induced the other party to make the contract.

Notice that in an **actionable misrepresentation** the statement must be one of fact, and not one of mere opinion, and that the untrue statement must induce the other party to make the contract. A party who checks the truth of a statement, and fails to discover that it is untrue, cannot claim to have been induced by it.

! Don't be tempted to . . .

You should not think that silence can never amount to an actionable misrepresentation. Generally, silence cannot be an actionable misrepresentation. However, it can in the following circumstances:

- where there has been a change of circumstances and this has caused a previously true statement to become untrue;
- in contracts of insurance, where all material facts must be disclosed;
- if there is a fiduciary relationship between the parties (for examples of fiduciary relationships see the relationships in which undue influence is presumed, later in this chapter [on p. 54]);
- if the silence makes a statement misleading.

Types of misrepresentation

There are three main types of **actionable misrepresentation**.

KEY DEFINITION: Misrepresentation – fraudulent, negligent and wholly innocent

A fraudulent misrepresentation is one which was made either knowing that it was false, or without belief in its truth, or recklessly careless as to whether it was true or false.

A negligent misrepresentation under s. 2(1) of the Misrepresentation Act 1967 is one made honestly believing that it was true by a person who cannot prove that he or she had reasonable grounds for this belief.

A wholly innocent misrepresentation is one made honestly believing that it was true by a person who can prove that he or she had reasonable grounds for this belief.

The burden of proof

A high standard of proof is required to establish that a misrepresentation was fraudulent, because an allegation of fraud is a serious charge to make. For this reason, a person to whom a **fraudulent misrepresentation** has been made often brings a claim for **negligent misrepresentation**.

> ✓ Make your answer stand out
>
> Show that you understand that the shifting burden of proof is one of the key differences between a negligent misrepresentation under s. 2(1) of the Misrepresentation Act 1967 and a wholly innocent misrepresentation. If a party alleges any type of misrepresentation, then the burden of proof will be on that party to prove that an actionable misrepresentation has been made. When a claim is brought under s. 2(1) of the MA 1967 the burden of proof will then shift onto the party who made the misrepresentation. If the misrepresentor can prove that he or she had reasonable grounds for believing that the facts represented were true, then the misrepresentation will be a wholly innocent misrepresentation. If he or she cannot prove this, the misrepresentation will be a negligent misrepresentation.

> **REVISION NOTE**
>
> A fourth type of action, suing for negligent misstatement at common law (see p. 85), is rarely argued. It needs the claimant to prove that there was a 'special relationship' between the parties; the burden of proving negligence is on the claimant and any damages will be for negligence rather than for the tort of deceit. For these reasons a claim under s. 2(1) of the MA 1967 is almost always preferable.

Remedies for misrepresentation

All three types of misrepresentation allow the injured party to rescind or avoid the contract. However, the contract is valid until it is avoided. Rescission in this context does not mean the same as rescission under Part 5A of the SGA 1979, considered in the previous chapter. Rescission here means calling off the contract, so that the parties are returned to the positions they were in before the contract was made.

> **EXAM TIP**
>
> Make sure that you explain the difference between a contract being void and being voidable. A contract which can be rescinded for misrepresentation is said to be voidable. It can be avoided by letting the other contracting party know that it is no longer binding. If this is not possible then, in the case of a fraudulent misrepresentation at least, it can be avoided by doing an act which shows a definite intention not to be bound by the contract. This is quite different from a contract being void. A void contract is no contract and so it confers no rights on anyone.

KEY CASE

***Car & Universal Finance Co Ltd* v. *Caldwell* [1965] 1 QB 525 (CA)**

Concerning: how a contract can be avoided

Facts

A man took a stolen cheque in exchange for his car. This was a fraudulent misrepresentation because the rogue impliedly stated that the cheque was good. Telling the police and AA to look out for the car was enough to avoid the contract.

Legal principle

In the case of a fraudulent misrepresentation, showing a definite intention not to be bound by the contract is enough to avoid the contract when it is not possible to find the misrepresentor. However, the Court of Appeal declined to say whether this would be enough if the misrepresentation was not fraudulent.

The right to rescind can be lost in the following ways:

- if the contract is affirmed;
- if a third party has acquired rights in the subject matter of the contract;
- if it is not possible to restore the parties to their pre-contract positions.

Affirmation arises when a party who knows that there has been a misrepresentation indicates that the contract will not be rescinded. It can sometimes arise by lapse of time; but as regards fraudulent misrepresentation mere lapse of time will not prevent rescission before the fraud has been discovered.

Both fraudulent and negligent misrepresentation under s. 2(1) of the MA 1967 allow the injured party to claim damages for the tort of deceit. Damages for the tort of deceit compensate for all losses and expenses caused by the deceit, even if these were not foreseeable. A wholly innocent misrepresentation gives no right to damages. However, it is possible for a court to award damages instead of rescission where it would be 'equitable to do so'. The courts do this very rarely.

EXAM TIP

Explain the two major advantages of negligent misrepresentation under s. 2(1) of the MA 1967. First, the remedies are essentially the same as for fraudulent misrepresentation, which is very hard to prove. Second, s. 2(1) puts the burden of proof on the misrepresentor to prove that he or she had reasonable grounds for believing that his or her statement was true.

Mistake

Common mistake

A **common mistake** can be made as to the following matters:

- the existence of the subject matter of the contract;
- the possibility of performing the contract;
- the quality of the subject matter of the contract.

A common mistake as to the ownership of goods will not make a contract void. See s. 12(1) of the SGA 1979 in Chapter 2 (on p. 26)

KEY DEFINITION: Common mistake

A common mistake occurs when the parties to the contract reach an agreement but do so while they are both making the same fundamental mistake.

Effect of common mistake

A common mistake as to existence, or as to the possibility of performance, will make a contract void. But a common mistake as to quality will generally not make a contract void.

KEY CASE

***Bell* v. *Lever Bros Ltd* [1932] AC 161 (HL)**

Concerning: when a common mistake as to quality will make a contract void

Facts

A company paid an employee £30,000 in order to make him redundant. Unknown to both parties, the employee could have been dismissed without any payment because he had breached the company's rules. So both parties thought that what was being bought, the right to dismiss the employee, was worth about £30,000 when in fact it was worth nothing. The contract was not void for mistake as to quality as the mistake was not sufficiently fundamental.

Legal principle

A common mistake as to quality of the subject matter of the contract will make the contract void only if the subject matter of the contract was essentially different from what the parties thought it was.

Lord Atkin said:

> A buys a picture from B; both A and B believe it to be the work of an old master, and a high price is paid. It turns out to be a modern copy. A has no remedy in the absence of a representation or [a term].

Great Peace Shipping Ltd v. *Tsavliris Salvage International Ltd* (2002) held that a mistake as to quality cannot make a contract voidable in equity. Earlier cases had suggested that it could.

Unilateral mistake

This may mean that no agreement was ever reached. So any 'contract' which seems to have been formed will be void. A **unilateral mistake** may invalidate a contract in the following ways:

- the offer and acceptance were ambiguous, so that it could not objectively be said what was agreed;
- the offeree was mistaken as to the terms which were being offered, and the offeror knew this;
- one party was mistaken as to the identity of the other contracting party.

The first two of these are essentially matters of fact and will depend upon the facts of each individual case. Mistake as to identity needs to be examined in more detail.

KEY DEFINITION: Unilateral mistake

When there is a unilateral mistake only one of the parties to the contract makes a mistake.

Mistake as to identity

A mistake as to the identity of the other contracting party can make a contract void, but only if the following three conditions are satisfied:

1. The parties must not have met face to face.
2. The mistake must have been as to the identity of the other party and not merely as to that party's attributes.
3. The mistake must be a material mistake, that is to say it must have mattered.

KEY CASE

***Cundy* v. *Lindsay* (1878) 3 App Cas 459 (HL)**

Concerning: when a mistake as to the person will make a contract void

Facts

A rogue knew that the claimants, manufacturers of handkerchiefs, had previously supplied a customer called Blenkiron. So the rogue hired premises close to Blenkiron's address and sent a letter ordering handkerchiefs to be delivered to this address. He ▶

also disguised his signature to look like Blenkiron's. The manufacturers sent handkerchiefs to Blenkiron at the rogue's hired premises. The rogue got possession of the handkerchiefs and sold 3,000 of them to the defendants.

Legal principle

Where the parties do not meet face to face, a material mistake as to identity will make the contract void. So the claimants got the handkerchiefs back because the contract was void for mistake. No ownership passed to the rogue and so he could not pass ownership to the defendants.

KEY CASE

***King's Norton Metal Co Ltd* v. *Edridge Merrett & Co Ltd* (1897) 14 TLR 98 (CA)**

Concerning: when a mistake as to the person will make a contract void

Facts

A rogue ordered goods from a manufacturer by letter, using very impressive notepaper which seemed to come from an impressive company. In fact the company did not exist at all. The rogue received the goods and sold them to the defendants.

Legal principle

Where the parties do not meet face to face and one party is mistaken only as to the attributes of the other contracting party, rather than as to that party's identity, the contract will not be void for mistake. So the mistake did not make the contract void, and the manufacturer contracted with the person who wrote the letter, the rogue. Having got ownership, the rogue passed ownership to the defendants.

The facts of the two cases are very similar. The key difference is that in *Cundy* the claimants thought that they knew the identity of the person they were dealing with. They thought they were dealing with Blenkiron, their previous customer. Whereas in *King's Norton* the claimants were mistaken only as to the attributes of who they were dealing with. They knew nothing of the rogue's fictitious company. They thought they were dealing with the person who wrote the letter, whom they took to be creditworthy.

! Don't be tempted to . . .

You should not think that the law in this area is settled. In *Shogun Finance Ltd* v. *Hudson* (2003) the House of Lords approved both of these decisions. However, two Lords in the minority thought that *Cundy* v. *Lindsay* should be overruled so that a contract was created with the rogue. So *Shogun Finance* did not change the law but you should be aware that it has raised the possibility of the law being changed in the future.

REVISION NOTE

In both of these cases, and in all cases where a rogue's lies induce a person to make a contract, the contract will be *voidable* for fraudulent misrepresentation. However, this is of no use to the claimant where the goods have been sold on to an innocent third party. Once this has happened the right to rescind will be lost because the third party will have acquired rights in the subject matter of the contract which would be affected by rescission. (See above in relation to misrepresentation.) That is why the innocent party tries to make the contract void for mistake. If the contract is *void* it is of no effect at all and so the goods can still be recovered from an innocent third-party purchaser. Ownership will never have passed to the rogue and so will never have passed from the rogue. So if you get an exam question on mistake as to the person where the contract is not void do not forget to go on to consider misrepresentation. (See, for example, *Car & Universal Finance Co Ltd* v. *Caldwell* (1965).)

The right to sue the rogue

Where an innocent owner of goods sells them to a rogue, and the rogue then sells them to an innocent third party, either the original owner or the innocent third party will not end up with ownership of the goods. The loser will have a remedy against the rogue. The seller can claim for fraudulent misrepresentation. The buyer can claim under s. 12(1) SGA (see p. 26). However, this is of little use if the rogue cannot be found or has no money.

Mistake as to what is being signed (*non est factum*)

If a person signs a document, while making a fundamental mistake as to the type of document which is being signed, the contract will be void for a type of mistake known as ***non est factum***, which means 'it is not my deed'. A person who is careless in signing a document cannot rely on *non est factum*.

KEY CASE

***Saunders* v. *Anglia Building Society* [1970] AC 1004 (HL)**

Concerning: the requirements of non est factum

Facts

A man tricked his elderly aunt into signing a document which immediately gave her house away. He told his aunt that the document gave the house away after her death, but that she would be allowed to live there for the rest of her life. The aunt signed the document without reading it because her glasses were broken.

Legal principle

Non est factum will apply only where the document signed was of a fundamentally different character from what the person thought they were signing. So here the contract was not void for *non est factum*.

Duress

Traditionally the common law doctrine of duress would make a contract voidable only if a person was forced into making it by the threat of unlawful, physical violence. More recently a doctrine of economic duress has arisen. Under this doctrine a person can also avoid a contract if he or she was pushed into it in such a way that there was no real consent, even if there was no threat of physical violence.

Undue influence

This is an equitable doctrine under which a contract can be voidable because one of the parties unduly influenced the other into making it. The party alleging undue influence must first prove that trust and confidence was placed in the other party. In the following relationships this is presumed:

- doctor and patient;
- solicitor and client;
- parent and child;
- guardian and ward;
- trustee and beneficiary;
- religious adviser and disciple.

Outside these relationships, it is necessary for the person alleging undue influence to prove that there actually was a relationship of trust and confidence.

The next step is that the person alleging undue influence must prove that there was a transaction which calls for explanation. If this is proved, the other party will have to prove that there was no undue influence. One way of proving this is to show that the party alleging undue influence took independent legal advice before making the contract.

Illegal contracts

The following types of contract are illegal on grounds of public policy and are therefore unenforceable:

- contracts tending to promote corruption in public life;
- contracts tending to impede the administration of justice;
- contracts to trade with enemy nations in time of war;

- contracts to commit a tort, crime or fraud;
- contracts tending to promote sexual immorality;
- contracts to defraud Revenue & Customs.

Contracts in restraint of trade

Contracts in restraint of trade attempt to prevent a person from working or from carrying on a business. They are void unless they can be proved to be reasonable. The only grounds upon which they can be reasonable are that they attempt to protect trade secrets, trade connections or confidential information. Even then, they must not be too wide in their scope. If an offending clause can be struck out without affecting the meaning of the rest of the contract, the rest of the contract will stand. If this cannot be done the whole contract will be void.

Contractual capacity of minors

A **minor** is defined by s. 1 of the Family Law Reform Act 1969 as a person who is under 18 years of age. Contracts made by minors might be valid, voidable or void, depending upon the type of contract made.

Valid contracts

The following will be considered valid:

- contracts for necessary goods (for which a reasonable price must be paid);
- contracts for necessary services;
- beneficial contracts of employment.

Voidable contracts

These include contracts of continuing obligation, such as:

- contracts of partnership;
- contracts to buy shares;
- contracts to take leases of land.

Void contracts

Contracts which are not classed as valid or voidable will be void.

Privity of contract

The concept of **privity** holds that a contract is private between the parties who created it. The contract cannot be enforced by anyone else and neither can it impose a burden on anybody else. This is the position at common law, except that certain consumer contracts made specifically to benefit third parties, such as the booking of a holiday or a taxi, might allow such a third party to claim damages if the contract is breached.

Contracts (Rights of Third Parties) Act 1999

The CRTPA 1999 can allow a third party to enforce a contract or part of a contract. It sets out two routes which a third party can take.

EXAM TIP

There are few significant cases on the Act yet. Be aware of the two routes and be ready, with examples, to demonstrate the effect of s. 1(1)(a), s. 1(1)(b), s. 1(2) and s. 1(3).

First, the s. 1(1)(a) route, which applies if the contract expressly provided that a third party could enforce it or parts of it. All that is then required is that s. 1(3) is satisfied. Section 1(3) requires that the third party is expressly identified.

Second, the s. 1(1)(b) route, which applies if the contract purported to confer a benefit on a third party. This route is used where the contract did not expressly provide that the third party could enforce the contract. After s. 1(1)(b) has been satisfied, the third party must next satisfy s. 1(2), which provides that the third party will still not be able to enforce the contract if it appeared that the parties did not intend him or her to be able to enforce it. After s. 1(2) has been satisfied, s. 1(3) must be satisfied.

EXAM TIP

Show awareness of the policy behind s. 1(2). If a contract does not expressly provide that a third party can enforce it, it would be absurd to allow a third party to enforce it just because it happened to confer a benefit upon him or her. For example, if a contractor agreed to build a new road for a local authority, but failed to do so, then the local authority could sue him or her for breach of contract. But if there was no s. 1(2), any motorist who would have used the new road would also have a right to sue.

Figure 3.1

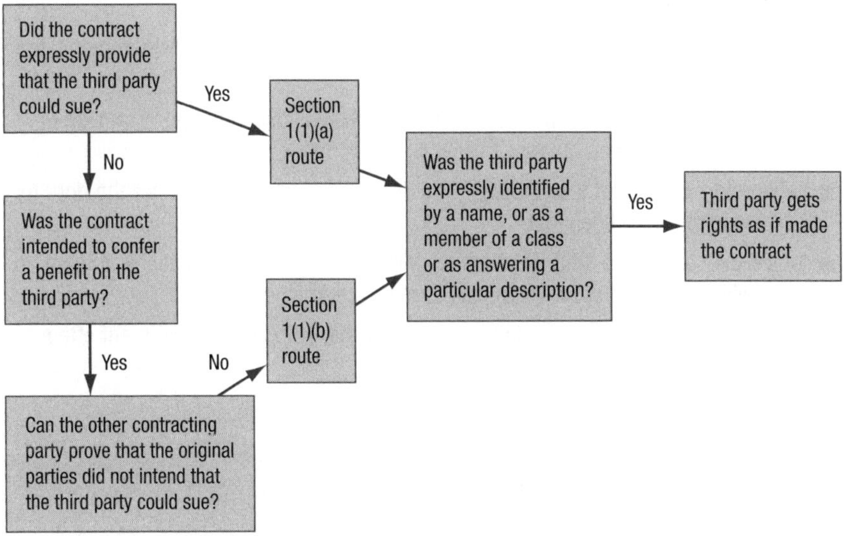

Putting it all together

Answer guidelines

See the problem question at the start of the chapter. This is a typical problem question on mistake as to the person. If you master this answer, most questions on this subject are likely to be easy.

Approaching the question

This question covers two areas of law, misrepresentation and mistake as to the person. Structure your answer logically. First, deal with fraudulent misrepresentation. Then consider mistake as to the person. Clearly explain the difference between a contract being void or being voidable, which is crucial to this answer. Apply cases to give authority to your answer. Don't forget to advise the party who does not get the car of any rights he or she may have against the rogue. ▶

Important points to include

- Did the rogue make a misrepresentation? To decide this you will need to apply the definition of an actionable misrepresentation.
- What remedies might be available to Jacek? This will depend upon what type of misrepresentation was made.
- When did Jacek avoid the contract? You will need to consider whether the right to rescind might have been lost.
- Could the contract be void for mistake? Mistake as to the person seems to be a possibility, but will it apply if the parties met face to face?
- Is the contract void, or voidable? Clearly show that you know the different effect of the contract being void and it being voidable.

✓ Make your answer stand out

There is a huge difference between a contract being void and it being voidable, as we have seen. Should a mistake as to the person ever make a contract void, or is the approach taken by the minority of the House of Lords in *Shogun Finance* better policy? Think of the situation where a rogue gets goods from their owner, without meeting the owner face to face, and sells the goods to a third party. Who is more at fault, the original owner of the goods or the third party? Who gets the goods, as the law now stands?

READ TO IMPRESS

Koh, P. (2008) Some Issues in Misrepresentation, 2 JBL 123–38

MacMillan, C. (2005) Rogues, Swindlers and Cheats: The Development of Mistake of Identity in English Contract Law, 64(3) CLJ 711–44

Palmer, E. (1991) The Fiction of Fraud, 141(6533) NLJ 1732–3

www.pearsoned.co.uk/lawexpress

Go online to access more revision support including quizzes to test your knowledge, sample questions with answer guidelines, podcasts you can download, and more!

Contract 4: Discharge of contractual obligations and remedies

4

Revision checklist

Essential points you should know:

- ☐ How a contract is discharged by performance
- ☐ How a contract is discharged by agreement
- ☐ How a contract is discharged by frustration
- ☐ How a contract is discharged by breach
- ☐ The remedies available for breach of contract

Topic map

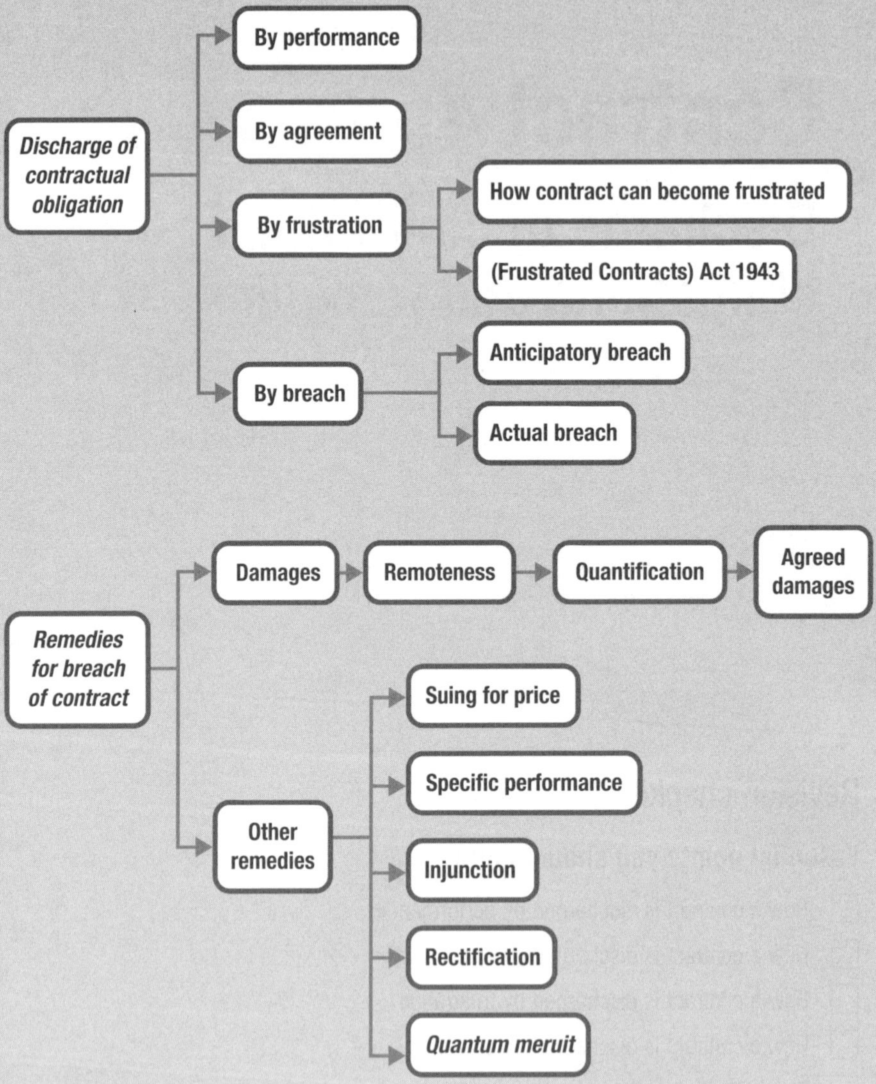

A printable version of this topic map is available from **www.pearsoned.co.uk/lawexpress**

Introduction

This area of contract law is often overlooked but it features in many exam questions.

Discharge of contractual obligations deals with the ways in which contractual obligations cease to exist. A remedy for breach of contract will be available whenever a term of a contract is breached. However, if the breach causes no loss, only nominal damages will be awarded.

ASSESSMENT ADVICE

Read the question. Is it about discharge, or remedies, or both? Is it about just one method by which a contract might be discharged, or several? Should more than one remedy be considered?

Don't forget that a question on a different topic, such as offer and acceptance or exclusion clauses, might also require you to deal with remedies. Whenever a contract is breached remedies should be considered unless the question indicates otherwise.

Sample question

Could you answer this question? Below is a typical problem question that could arise on this topic. Guidelines on answering the question are included at the end of this chapter, while a sample essay question and guidance on tackling it can be found on the companion website.

PROBLEM QUESTION

Box Ltd manufactures cardboard boxes. Sparks Ltd agreed to install electrical wiring in Box Ltd's new factory, so that machines and lights could be used. The contract stated that this work would be finished by 1 June. Sparks Ltd could not complete the work until 1 October because two of their key employees left their jobs. Consequently, Box Ltd were unable to run their new factory until 1 October. Box Ltd are now suing for breach of contract, claiming damages in respect of the following losses: lost profits of £40,000; damages of £17,000 which became payable to one of their customers when cardboard boxes which they had ordered were not delivered; and £32,000 which the general manager of Box Ltd spent on private healthcare. This healthcare expenditure was incurred on account of the stress caused by Sparks Ltd's breach of contract.

Advise Box Ltd of their legal position. How would your advice differ, if at all, if the contract between Box Ltd and Sparks Ltd had said that in the event of late completion by Sparks Ltd the damages payable would be £6,000 a week?

Discharge of contractual obligations

The terms of a contract impose obligations on the parties, as we saw in Chapter 2. When these obligations are discharged they cease to exist. This can happen in four ways:

1. by performance;
2. by agreement;
3. by frustration or;
4. by breach.

Discharge by performance of the contract

Almost all contracts cease to exist when the parties fully perform their contractual obligations. Difficulties arise when one party does not fully perform. If a party's obligations are discharged that party can withhold performance of his or her obligations without being in breach of contract.

EXAM TIP

Remember that discharge of contractual obligations is about whether or not a party still has to perform the contract. It is not about whether a claim for damages can be made. Any breach of contract allows the injured party to claim damages.

When an offer of a unilateral contract is made the offeror promises to do something if the other party performs some act. Only if that act is fully performed must the offeror do what was promised.

REVISION NOTE

The difference between unilateral and bilateral contracts was considered in Chapter 1.

In bilateral contracts the *general rule* is also that if one party fails to entirely perform the contract the other party need not perform at all. Most of the cases are concerned with whether any payment must be made for partially performed services. This is because when goods are sold the SGA 1979 classifies the seller's duties under the contract as conditions.

As we saw in Chapter 2, if a condition is breached the injured party can terminate the contract. The general rule is subject to the following exceptions.

A *severable contract* consists of several independent obligations. A party who performs only some of these can claim some of the other party's consideration, but will remain liable in damages for the obligations not performed. So the injured party's contractual obligations are not fully discharged by the other party's failure fully to perform. Whether or not a contract is severable depends upon the intentions of the parties.

A party who very nearly completes all of the contractual obligations is said to have made *substantial performance*. That party can insist that the other party performs the contract, but will remain liable in damages for failing to fully perform his or her own obligations.

Voluntary acceptance of partial performance allows for a claim on a ***quantum meruit***, a remedy explained later in this chapter.

Prevention of performance by one contracting party allows the party who was prevented from performing to claim on a *quantum meruit*.

Discharge by agreement

The parties assume obligations when they make the contract. They are free to make a second contract under which they agree to discharge each other from their obligations under the original contract. As this second agreement must be another contract, both parties must give some consideration to the other. This causes problems when one party has fully performed, and therefore has no more obligations, and agrees that the other party need not perform some or all of his or her obligations. Such an agreement will not be a contract, because of the lack of consideration, and will therefore not be binding.

REVISION NOTE

A contract is discharged by agreement only if a new contract is made. Discharge by agreement is therefore about formation of contracts, a subject considered in Chapter 1.

A party who waives his or her rights indicates that he or she will not insist upon them. If no consideration is given in return for a waiver of contractual rights the contract is not discharged. However, the rights surrendered can be reintroduced only by giving reasonable notice.

Discharge by frustration

A contract will be frustrated if it *becomes*:

- impossible to perform; or
- illegal to perform;
- radically different from what the parties contemplated.

EXAM TIP

Remember that frustration is concerned only with contracts which become illegal, etc. A contract which is illegal, when it is made, is void. A contract which, when it is made, is impossible to perform or is radically different from what the parties intended may be void for mistake. (Illegality and mistake were both considered in Chapter 3.)

Impossibility of performance

A contract which becomes impossible to perform will be frustrated. For example, if a person agreed to provide services personally, and died before the services had been performed, the contract would be frustrated.

Illegality of performance

A contract which becomes illegal to perform will be frustrated. This happened in the *Fibrosa Case* (1943) when a contract to supply goods to Poland became illegal when Germany, a nation with which the UK was at war, occupied Poland.

The contract becomes radically different

A contract will be frustrated if it becomes radically different from what the parties contemplated when they made the contract. However, it can be difficult to say when a contract has become radically different.

KEY CASE

***Krell* v. *Henry* [1903] 2 KB 740 (CA)**

Concerning: the circumstances in which a contract will be frustrated

Facts

A room in Pall Mall was hired for two days for £75. The sole purpose of this was to watch the coronation procession of the King, which would pass by the room. The contract did not mention this purpose. The King was ill and so the procession was cancelled.

Legal principle

A contract will be frustrated if its foundation has become radically different from what the parties contemplated when they made the contract. Here the foundation of the contract, viewing the procession, had become radically different. So the contract was frustrated.

KEY CASE

***Herne Bay Steamboat Co* v. *Hutton* [1903] 2 KB 683 (CA)**

Concerning: the circumstances in which a contract will be frustrated

Facts

A contract was made to hire a steamboat for two days 'for the purpose of viewing the naval review and for a day's cruise around the fleet'. The naval review was cancelled because the King was ill.

Legal principle

The contract was not frustrated because the foundation of the contract, hiring the boat, had not become radically different.

! Don't be tempted to . . .

You should not think that these two cases disagree with each other. They can be hard to reconcile but the same judges sat in both cases. In *Herne Bay* the contract was not frustrated because it would still have been possible to perform a significant purpose of the contract and so the foundation of the contract was not radically different. In *Krell* v. *Henry* the foundation of the contract had been destroyed because both parties knew that there was no purpose at all in hiring the rooms if the procession did not take place. However, in many other situations it can be difficult to decide which case is more applicable. If in doubt you should apply both of these cases.

Limits on frustration

EXAM TIP

Frustration is very much a doctrine of last resort. A court will not easily find a contract frustrated. So be aware of the limits on frustration.

A contract will not be frustrated if:

- it merely becomes more difficult to perform;
- a *force majeure* clause is effective;
- the 'frustrating' event was foreseeable;
- the 'frustrating' event was self-induced.

If a term of a contract states that the contract must be performed in a particular way then it will be frustrated if it becomes impossible to perform in that particular way. But a contract will not become frustrated merely because it becomes more difficult to perform. So if a contract states that goods must be carried via a particular route, it will be frustrated if carriage via that route becomes impossible. But if no term stated that the goods would be carried by that particular route it would not be frustrated if this became impossible, as long as the goods could be carried by a different route.

A ***force majeure clause*** in a contract sets out what should happen if unexpected difficulties should arise. Such clauses are given legal effect. So if the difficulties envisaged do arise the contract will not be frustrated because the *force majeure* clause will be applied.

A party who foresees, or should have foreseen, a particular event cannot claim that this event frustrates the contract.

A party who brought about an event which would ordinarily frustrate the contract cannot claim that the event has frustrated the contract. The 'frustrating' event is said to be 'self-induced'.

KEY CASE

***Maritime National Fish Ltd* v. *Ocean Trawlers Ltd* [1935] AC 524 (PC)**

Concerning: whether frustrating event was self-induced

Facts

The claimants chartered a boat to the defendants. The ship was fitted with a certain type of fishing net and both parties knew that it was illegal to fish with such a net unless the Canadian government issued a licence. The defendants had four other boats fitted with such nets, so they applied for five licences. They were granted only three. They assigned these three licences to their own boats and claimed that their contract with the claimants was frustrated.

Legal principle

A party whose actions bring about an event cannot claim that that event frustrated a contract. So the contract was not frustrated.

The legal effect of frustration

The contract comes to an end as soon as the frustrating event occurs. Then the Law Reform (Frustrated Contracts) Act 1943 makes the following rules:

- Money owing under the contract ceases to be payable.
- Money either paid or payable at the time of the frustrating event is recoverable. However, the court has a discretion to allow some of this money to be retained to cover expenses incurred.
- If one of the parties to the contract has received a valuable benefit under the contract, the court can order that a fair amount is paid to compensate for this. The case law suggests that this benefit should be valued immediately *after* the frustrating event.

EXAM TIP

Remember that the LRFCA 1943 is not concerned with how a contract becomes frustrated; it is concerned only with the consequences of frustration.

Discharge by breach

Sometimes a breach of contract by one party will allow the other party to treat his or her contractual obligations as discharged.

REVISION NOTE

In Chapter 2 we considered conditions, warranties and innominate terms, and the extent to which one party's breach allows the other party to treat the contract as terminated. This area was concerned with whether an actual breach of contract allows the injured party to regard contractual obligations as discharged. If an exam question concerns an actual breach, apply the rules set out in Chapter 2.

Anticipatory breach

A party faced with an **anticipatory breach** has two options: first, to accept the anticipatory breach. This will mean that the contract is immediately terminated, that neither party will have to perform their contractual obligations, and that the injured party can sue for damages. Second, the injured party can keep the contract open and wait to see if the other party actually does perform. If the other party does perform, the right to sue for the anticipatory breach will be lost. If the other party does not perform, the anticipatory breach will have become an actual breach and the injured party can sue for breach of contract. Acceptance of an anticipatory breach must be clearly made or the contract will remain alive.

KEY DEFINITION: Anticipatory breach

An anticipatory breach occurs when, before performance of the contract is due, one of the parties makes it plain to the other party that the contract will not be performed.

EXAM TIP

There is a danger in not accepting an anticipatory breach. If the contract becomes frustrated after the anticipatory breach, but before this becomes an actual breach, the right to sue for breach of contract will have been lost. You should look out for this possibility.

Legislation giving the right to cancel concluded contracts

The Consumer Protection (Cancellation of Contracts made in a Consumer's Home or Place of Work etc.) Regulations 2008 allow consumers to cancel contracts if two conditions are satisfied. First, the contract must have been made during a visit by a trader to a consumer's home or place of work. Second, the contract must have been to provide goods or services costing more than £35. The trader cannot enforce the contract unless the consumer was given written notice of the right to cancel within fourteen days and a statutory cancellation form.

KEY INSTRUMENT

Consumer Protection (Distance Selling) Regulations 2000

The CPDS Regs 2000 give consumers who buy goods or services by means of a distance contract a fourteen-day cooling-off period. A contract is a distance contract if it is concluded without the consumer and the supplier ever actually meeting each other. During the cooling-off period the contract can be cancelled by the consumer.

The Consumer Credit Act 1974 allows a debtor to cancel a regulated consumer credit agreement within 14 days of making it, without giving any reason. However, the right to cancel the credit agreement does not allow cancellation of contracts to buy goods or services which were to be paid for with the credit.

Remedies for breach of contract

Refusal to perform the contract

The circumstances in which one party can refuse to perform future contractual obligations, on account of a breach of contract by the other party, have already been considered. (See conditions, warranties and innominate terms in Chapter 2 and 'Discharge by performance' in this chapter.)

Damages

Any breach of contract gives rise to a right to sue for damages. **Nominal damages** (token damages) can be claimed merely because a contract has been breached. However, substantial damages can be claimed only for an identified loss, which was caused by the breach of contract, and which was not too remote.

Remoteness of damage

The two rules in *Hadley* v. *Baxendale* (1854) limit the losses for which damages can be claimed:

- Rule 1 allows damages to be recovered for a loss if the loss arose naturally from the breach of contract, in the usual course of things.
- Rule 2 allows damages for other losses to be recoverable if the loss can reasonably be supposed to have been in the contemplation of the parties when they made the contract.

Losses which are outside the two rules are regarded as too remote and no damages can be claimed in respect of them.

KEY CASE

***Victoria Laundry Ltd* v. *Newman Industries Ltd* [1949] 2 KB 528 (CA)**

Concerning: application of the two rules in Hadley *v.* Baxendale

Facts

The defendants sold a new boiler to a laundry. They breached the contract by delivering 20 weeks late. The laundry claimed £16 a week for the extra profit they could have made by doing more general laundry work with the new boiler. They also claimed £262 a week, this amount having been lost on account of the laundry not being able to perform a special contract to dye army uniforms.

Legal principle

The £16 a week was recoverable under Rule 1. The £262 a week was not recoverable. As it was not within either rule, it was too remote.

EXAM TIP

The two rules in *Hadley* v. *Baxendale* must be applied when answering problem questions on damages. The actual decision in *Victoria Laundry* provides examples of Rule 1 applying (to the claim for £16 a week) and of neither rule applying (to the claim for £262 a week). The case can also be used to demonstrate Rule 2. If the laundry had told the defendants about the special contract, before the contract to sell the boiler was made, then the loss would have been recoverable under Rule 2.

Amount of damages

The general purpose of contract damages is to put injured parties in the economic position which they would have been in if the contract had been properly performed. So, subject to the rules on causation and remoteness, damages can be claimed for matters such as loss of profit, damages which become payable to a third party and the cost of putting right defects caused by the breach of contract.

Special rules in contracts for sale of goods

KEY STATUTE

Sale of Goods Act 1979, s. 51(2)

If a seller of goods does not deliver the goods, s. 51(2) of the SGA 1979 provides that the damages are assessed under *Hadley* v. *Baxendale*, in the normal way, unless *there is an available market* for the goods. If there is an available market, the damages are assessed as the market price of the goods on the date when they should have been delivered minus the contract price. There will be an available market for goods if they were not unique, if a different seller could be found and if the price of such goods could be fixed by supply and demand.

Mitigation

A party who has suffered a loss as a result of breach of contract must take all reasonable steps to mitigate the loss. Damages will not be claimable in respect of losses which could have been mitigated.

Injured feelings

Damages are generally not recoverable for injured feelings or distress. But if the whole purpose of the contract was to provide enjoyment and relaxation it is possible for damages to be claimed for disappointment and distress caused by a breach of the contract.

Agreed damages

Sometimes the contract itself states what the damages should be in the event of the contract being breached. Whether this agreement is given effect will depend upon whether the amount agreed was **liquidated damages** or a **penalty**. Liquidated damages are a 'genuine pre-estimate of the loss', that is to say they are the amount of loss which the parties thought the breach would cause. These liquidated damages are applied even if the loss was not the amount spelt out in the liquidated damages clause. Large sums which are designed to terrorise a party into performing a contract are not liquidated damages because they are not a genuine pre-estimate of the loss. They are known as penalties. The courts ignore such penalty clauses and assess damages in the usual way, as if the penalty clause had not existed. A large sum payable otherwise than upon a breach of contract cannot be struck out as a penalty.

✓ Make your answer stand out

Query whether penalties should be restricted to sums payable on breach of a contract.

What if a contract term says that the price for a service, such as servicing a car, is £2,000 which must be payable within one month but another term says that if full payment is made early, within two weeks, the price is £150? The customer sees the price as £150 because he or she intends to pay within two weeks. If payment is not made within two weeks, the price is £2,000. This is not a penalty because it was not breach of the contract which made it become payable. Should it be a penalty?

Suing for the contract price

Suing for the contract price is not the same as suing for damages. It is an action in debt because what is being claimed is the definite sum of money which is owed. As the action is not for damages, the rules on remoteness and mitigation do not apply.

Specific performance

This is an equitable remedy which requires a person actually to perform his or her contractual obligations. It is rarely ordered. It will not be ordered in the following circumstances:

- where damages would be a good enough remedy;
- in favour of a party who has behaved inequitably (unfairly);
- where it would cause undue hardship to the defendant;
- to enforce a contract which must be performed personally;
- either for or against a minor (person under 18 years of age).

Injunction

An injunction is a court order requiring a person to do or not to do a certain thing. It is possible to get an injunction to prevent a party from breaching a contractual obligation. However, an injunction will not be ordered where damages would provide a satisfactory remedy. Nor will an injunction be ordered in circumstances in which specific performance could not be ordered, if the injunction would have the same effect as specific performance.

Rectification

This is an equitable remedy which applies when the parties have made a contract orally and then write down what they have agreed. If they incorrectly record what was agreed, rectification can be allowed so that the written document is put right.

Quantum meruit (as much as is deserved)

A claim on a *quantum meruit* is a claim for payment of the amount deserved for work done. Such a claim can be made if:

- the other contracting party prevented further performance of the contract;
- the other contracting party voluntarily accepted partial performance of the contract;
- the contract did not provide how much should be paid. (Both the SGA 1979, in the case of a sale of goods, and the SGSA 1982, in the case of a contract to provide services, set out that a reasonable price should be paid.)

Time limits on remedies

The Limitation Act 1980 provides that a simple contract (one not made by deed) must be sued upon within six years of the right to sue arising. A claim for personal injuries must be made within three years. When a contract is made by deed it must be sued upon within 12 years of the right to sue arising.

Time runs against minors only after they reach the age of 18. Time does not run against a victim of fraud until the fraud is, or should have been, discovered.

Any written acknowledgement of a debt will cause the time period to begin again. The LA 1980 does not apply to equitable remedies. But these are lost fairly quickly through the doctrine of *laches* (delay).

Putting it all together

Answer guidelines

See the problem question at the start of the chapter.

Approaching the question

The question concerns whether or not the contract between Box Ltd and Sparks Ltd has been discharged by frustration or whether it has been breached. If it has been breached then remedies will be available. If it was frustrated the LRFCA 1943 would set out the legal position.

Important points to include

- Has there been a breach of contract, or was the contract frustrated? You should explain frustration but also explain the limits on the doctrine.
- If there was a breach can Box Ltd claim for the losses caused by the breach?
- Are the losses too remote? Consider each loss in turn.
- Could Box Ltd have mitigated any of the losses?
- If the damages were agreed at £6,000 a week, is this liquidated damages or a penalty? This will depend upon whether the agreed damages were a 'genuine pre-estimate' of the loss.

✓ Make your answer stand out

Apply rules in *Hadley* v. *Baxendale* to each of the losses.

READ TO IMPRESS

Liu, Q. (2006) Accepted Anticipatory Breach: Duty of Mitigation and Damages Assessment, 1 LMCLQ 17–22

Newman, P. (2007) Liquidated Damages, (June) CN 44–5

www.pearsoned.co.uk/lawexpress

Go online to access more revision support including quizzes to test your knowledge, sample questions with answer guidelines, podcasts you can download, and more!

5 Tort

Revision checklist

Essential points you should know:

- [ ] The differences between contractual and tortious liability
- [ ] The requirements of the tort of negligence
- [ ] The effect of the Consumer Protection Act 1987, Part 1
- [ ] An outline of the requirements of torts other than negligence
- [ ] The circumstances in which an employer can be liable for the torts of employees

Topic map

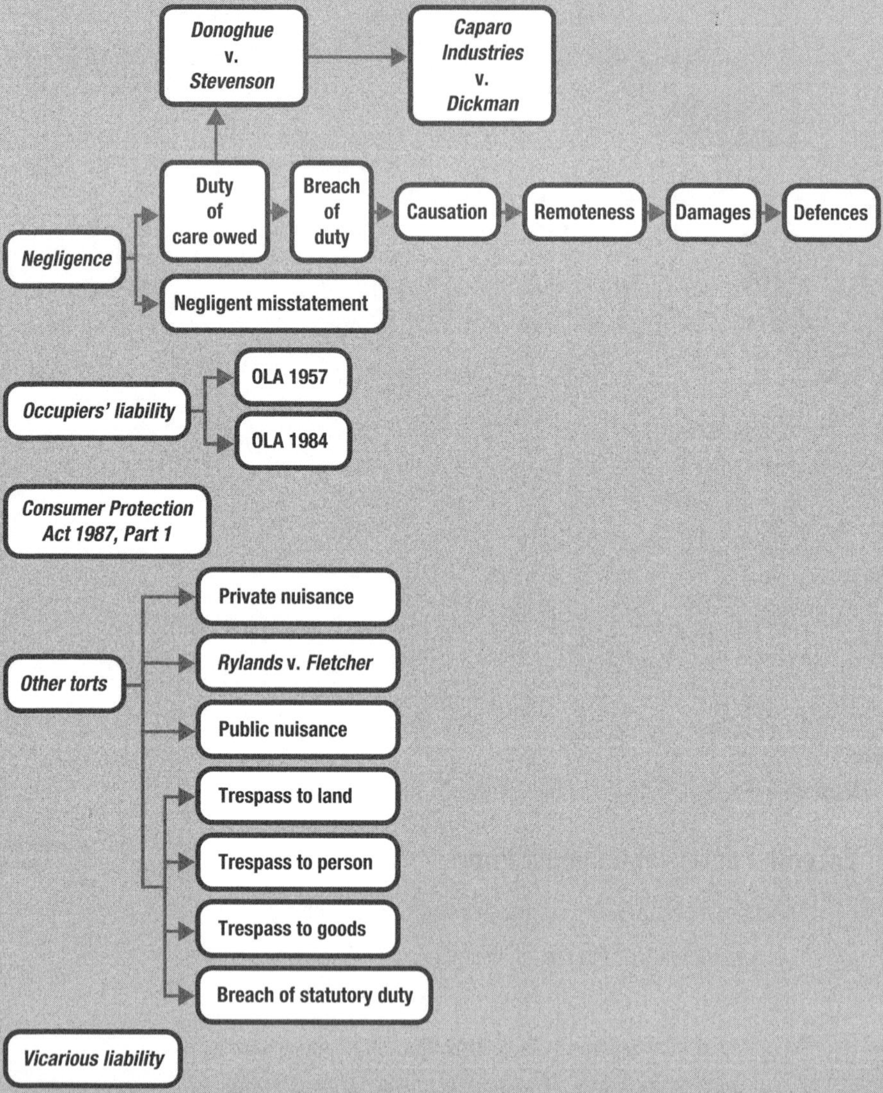

A printable version of this topic map is available from **www.pearsoned.co.uk/lawexpress**

Introduction

This chapter deals mainly with the tort of negligence, a subject which is the focus of many exam questions.

The chapter also considers other torts, in rather less detail, and distinguishes liability in tort from liability in contract.

ASSESSMENT ADVICE

Essay questions

Essay questions on negligence often require you to explain the requirements of the tort, along with defences and remedies, and to comment upon whether the law satisfactorily achieves justice. In questions such as this you must remember to give your opinion as to whether or not the law does satisfactorily achieve justice.

Problem questions

Approach a problem question on negligence in an organised way. First, establish whether the requirements of the tort have been satisfied. This may involve a detailed analysis of some of the requirements. Then see if any defences apply. Finally, if appropriate, consider remedies.

Sample question

Could you answer this question? Below is a typical problem question that could arise on this topic. Guidelines on answering the question are included at the end of this chapter, while a sample essay question and guidance on tackling it can be found on the companion website.

PROBLEM QUESTION

Recently Seema suffered a broken leg when out walking. The accident was caused by Ted, who was cycling on the pavement. Ted did not notice Seema and crashed his bike into her, causing the injury. Seema did not see Ted, although she was facing his direction, because at the time she was dialling a number on her mobile phone. ▶

As a result of the injury Seema could not work in her job as sales canvasser for two months, and so she lost two months' earnings. Seema's employer also lost about the same amount on account of Seema not working. The day after the accident Seema's mother, Anjana, used her new microwave, which a friend had bought her as a birthday present. The microwave exploded, injuring Anjana's arm and causing some damage to her kitchen. It has not been possible to discover why the microwave exploded.

Advise Seema, her employer, and Anjana of their legal positions.

Contract and tort distinguished

A tort is a civil wrong which is not a breach of contract. Liability in tort differs from contractual liability in the following ways:

- Contractual liability is assumed voluntarily, in return for the other party also assuming liability under the contract. Liability in tort is not undertaken voluntarily but is imposed by the courts.
- Liability in contract is generally strict, whereas liability in tort is almost always based on fault.
- Contract damages try to put the injured party into the position he or she would have been in if the contract had been properly performed. Tort damages try to put the injured party into the position he or she would have been in if the tort had never been committed.

Negligence

In order to establish the tort of negligence the claimant must prove three things, on a balance of probabilities:

1. that the defendant owed him or her a duty of care;
2. that the defendant breached that duty.
3. that this breach of duty caused a foreseeable type of damage.

Each of these requirements must be considered in detail.

A duty of care was owed

KEY CASE

***Donoghue* v. *Stevenson* [1932] AC 562 (HL)**

Concerning: when a duty of care is owed

Facts

The claimant's friend bought the claimant a bottle of ginger beer in a café. The ginger beer contained the remains of a decomposed snail. This caused the claimant to suffer nervous shock and food poisoning. The claimant had no contract with the café owner and so she sued the manufacturer of the ginger beer in negligence. It was held that if these facts could be proved the manufacturers would be liable in the tort of negligence.

Legal principle

A duty of care can be owed in a wide variety of circumstances. Lord Atkin gave a broad explanation of when a duty of care will be owed:

> You must take reasonable care to avoid acts and omissions which you can reasonably foresee would be likely to injure your neighbour. Who, then, in law is my neighbour? The answer seems to be – persons who are so closely and directly affected by my act that I ought reasonably to have them in contemplation as being so affected when I am directing my mind to the acts or omissions which are called in question.

Certain duty situations have become well established through case law. For example, road users owe a duty of care to other road users and pedestrians, manufacturers and repairers owe a duty of care to their customers, and professional advisers owe a duty of care to their clients. The true significance of *Donoghue* v. *Stevenson* is that it allows the tort of negligence to expand to cover new situations. However, when a new situation arises, the courts take an *incremental approach*. This means that they decide whether or not a duty of care is owed by considering how similar the new situation is to situations where the courts have already decided that duty is or is not owed.

KEY CASE

***Caparo Industries plc* v. *Dickman* [1990] 1 All ER 568 (HL)**

Concerning: extending a duty of care to new situations

Facts

The facts of this case are lengthy and complicated and to summarise them here would add little to an understanding of the legal principle outlined below. Remember that examiners are usually looking for an understanding of the *ratio* and legal principle and that reciting the facts in an exam will not improve your grade. ▶

Legal principle

A duty of care will be owed if three conditions are satisfied:

1 It must have been foreseeable that harm would be caused to the claimant.
2 There must have been 'proximity of relationship' between the claimant and the defendant.
3 It must be just and reasonable for the court to impose a duty of care.

Proximity is a complex matter which is closely connected with forseeability but which also considers the closeness of the relationship between the claimant and the defendant. The third step, that it is just and reasonable to impose a duty of care, is much more likely to be satisfied if the claimant has suffered physical injury, rather than economic loss or nervous shock.

Nervous shock

A duty of care can be owed in respect of psychiatric injury, which is generally known as 'nervous shock'. However, the courts are cautious in finding that such a duty exists. A duty not to cause nervous shock is owed to primary victims, such as people who also suffer physical injury. However, secondary victims, who were not themselves in danger of physical injury, are generally not owed a duty of care in respect of nervous shock, unless they had a very proximate relationship with a person who was physically injured.

Economic loss

Generally, there is no duty of care not to cause purely economic loss. Loss other than injury to the person or damage to property is regarded as economic loss. However, if economic loss is connected to a physical injury, or to damage to property, then a duty of care not to cause such loss will exist. So a person who is physically injured, and has to have time off work, can claim damages for lost wages. But in cases where the only loss suffered is economic loss, damages generally cannot be claimed. For example, in *Weller* v. *Foot and Mouth Research Institute* (1966) the defendants negligently allowed foot and mouth disease to escape from their laboratory. They were held not to be liable to a firm of livestock auctioneers who lost a lot of money on account of not being able to hold auctions until the disease was eradicated. The loss suffered by the auctioneers was pure economic loss.

The duty of care was breached

A duty of care will be breached if the defendant does not take the care which a reasonable person would take in all the circumstances. This is an *objective standard* and it is no defence that the defendant was doing his or her incompetent best. A higher standard of care is expected of professional people and people who claim to have some special competence. Professional people must show the degree of care which a reasonably competent person in that profession would show, and failure to show this standard will amount to breach of duty. There will have been no breach of a duty of care unless it could reasonably have been foreseen that the defendant's actions would cause injury.

In deciding whether or not a duty has been breached, the courts tend to attach particular importance to four factors:

1. the likelihood of the claimant suffering harm;
2. the potential seriousness of injury which the claimant was likely to suffer;
3. the cost of making sure that no harm was caused;
4. the usefulness of the defendant's actions.

The first two factors are weighed against the second two. If the first two are greater than the second two then it is likely that the duty will have been breached. If they are smaller it is likely that it will not.

Desirable activities and apologies

Sections 1 and 2 of the Compensation Act 2006 codified the existing common law.

KEY STATUTE

Compensation Act 2006, ss. 1 and 2

Deterrent effect of potential liability:

1 A court considering a claim in negligence or breach of statutory duty may, in determining whether the defendant should have taken particular steps to meet a standard of care (whether by taking precautions against a risk or otherwise), have regard to whether a requirement to take those steps might:

(a) prevent a desirable activity from being undertaken at all, to a particular extent or in a particular way, or

(b) discourage persons from undertaking functions in connection with a desirable activity.

2 An apology, an offer of treatment or other redress, shall not of itself amount to an admission of negligence or breach of statutory duty.

As these two sections codified the law they did not change the existing law. It was felt to be necessary to codify the law because some people wrongly believed that a person who caused another's injury would always be liable in negligence, and that an apology would automatically incur liability in negligence.

The thing speaks for itself (previously known as *res ipsa loquitur*)

As negligence is a civil action, the claimant must prove the case on a balance of probabilities. Sometimes the claimant will not be able to prove the precise way the defendant was negligent. By claiming that the thing speaks for itself, the claimant can *reverse the burden of proof*, so that the defendant must prove that the damage was not caused by his or her failure to take reasonable care.

The claimant will be able to say that the thing speaks for itself only if the following three conditions are satisfied:

1. the defendant must have been in control of the thing that caused the damage;
2. the accident must be the kind of accident which would not normally happen without negligence; and
3. the cause of the accident must be unknown.

Causation

In order to recover damages for the tort of negligence, the claimant must prove that the defendant's breach of duty caused the loss in respect of which damages are being claimed. Furthermore, the claimant must prove that the loss was a type of loss which would foreseeably follow from the defendant's breach.

To prove that the defendant caused the loss, the claimant must show that there was a chain of causation between the defendant's breach of duty and the claimant's loss. This chain must not be broken by a new act intervening (previously known as *novus actus interveniens*). Reflex actions will not break the chain of causation.

! Don't be tempted to . . .

Generally the courts apply a 'but for' test. So they ask whether, but for the defendant having breached the duty of care, the claimant would have suffered the injury in respect of which a claim is being made. However, the 'but for' test cannot cater for all situations. Difficulties arise where the claimant's loss was caused not only by the defendant's negligence but also by other causes.

KEY CASE

***McGhee* v. *National Coal Board* [1972] 3 All ER 1008 (HL)**

Concerning: multiple causes of injury

Facts

The claimant's employers asked him to clean out brick kilns. No washing facilities were provided even though the work was hot and dirty and exposed the claimant to clouds of brick dust. The claimant used to ride his bicycle home while caked with sweat and grime and soon developed dermatitis. This was caused by working in the kiln, but the risk of dermatitis was materially increased by the claimant cycling home without washing. The defendants were held liable in negligence.

Legal principle

A defendant is liable to a claimant if his breach of duty caused, or materially contributed to, the claimant's injury. This was the case even if there were other factors which contributed to the injury.

Foreseeability

Damages cannot be claimed for a loss unless the loss was a foreseeable consequence of the defendant's breach of duty. The extent of the loss does not need to be foreseeable, nor does the precise way in which it arose. However, the *type* of loss must have been foreseeable.

KEY CASE

***The Wagon Mound* [1961] AC 388 (PC)**

Concerning: foreseeability

Facts

The defendants negligently spilt a large quantity of furnace oil into Sydney Harbour. The claimants' wharf was burnt down when the oil caught fire. Normally this type of oil would not catch fire when lying on sea water. But a bale of cotton floating on the water was ignited by a spark from a welder's torch before sailing into the oil and setting it on fire. The defendants were held not to be liable for the damage which the fire caused.

Legal principle

A person who causes loss or injury through negligence will be liable only for loss or damage which was of a foreseeable type.

As long as a certain type of damage is forseeable, then the defendant will be liable for all damage of that type.

Defences to negligence

Contributory negligence

Contributory negligence is not a complete defence. Instead, it reduces the damages payable to the claimant.

KEY STATUTE

Law Reform (Contributory Negligence) Act 1945, s. 1

Where any person suffers damage as the result partly of his own fault and partly of the fault of any other person . . . the damages recoverable . . . shall be reduced to such an extent as the court thinks just and equitable having regard to the claimant's share in the responsibility for the damage.

Volenti non fit injuria (to one who volunteers no harm is done)

It is a complete defence to show that the injured person voluntarily assumed the risk which caused the injury. The defence is known by its Latin name, **volenti non fit injuria**. It often defeats employees who are injured as a result of not following safety procedures.

Exclusion of liability for negligence

REVISION NOTE

In Chapter 2, the Unfair Contract Terms Act 1977 was examined. It was seen that s. 2(1) of the Act provides that no contract term or notice can exclude or restrict liability for death or personal injury resulting from negligence. It was also seen that s. 2(2) provides that liability for loss or damage other than death or personal injury can be excluded, but only to the extent that this is reasonable. Section 2 applies to the tort of negligence, as well as to failure to take reasonable care in the performance of a contractual obligation. It also applies to the duty to take reasonable care imposed by the Occupiers' Liability Act 1957 (considered later in this chapter).

Damages

Damages for the tort of negligence are designed to put the injured party into the position he or she would have been in if the tort had not been committed.

Mitigation

A claimant has a duty to take all reasonable steps to mitigate (reduce) the loss suffered. Damages cannot be claimed for a loss which could have been mitigated by taking reasonable steps. However, if a reasonable attempt to mitigate the loss actually increases the loss, the claimant can recover damages to cover this increased loss.

EXAM TIP

When faced with a problem question on negligence, approach the question in the order in which this book approached it. First, establish that a duty was owed, that it was breached and that this caused a foreseeable type of damage. Second, consider any defences which might apply. Third, consider damages.

Negligent misstatement

Negligent misstatement is not a tort in its own right. It is a branch of the tort of negligence. But remember that liability for negligent misstatement can give rise to damages for economic loss.

KEY CASE

***Hedley Byrne & Co Ltd* v. *Heller and Partners Ltd* [1963] 2 All ER 575 (HL)**

Concerning: negligent misstatement

Facts

The facts of this case are lengthy and complicated and to summarise them here would add little to an understanding of the legal principle outlined below.

Legal principle

A duty of care not to cause loss by making a negligent misstatement can arise, but only if there is a special relationship between the parties. Where there is a special relationship the duty extends to not causing economic loss. There will be a special relationship only if the claimant could reasonably and foreseeably expect to be able to rely on the defendant's advice. There is no requirement that the defendant should receive anything in return for the advice. However, it is necessary that the claimant asked for the advice or had a right to receive it.

In *Caparo Industries plc* v. *Dickman* (1990) the House of Lords held that the relationship between individual members of a company and the company auditor was not close enough to amount to a special relationship. However, it was also held that the auditors do owe a duty of care to the company and to the company members as a whole.

Occupiers' liability

Occupiers of premises owe a duty of care to all **visitors**, and a separate duty of care to trespassers. Any person with control of premises can be liable as an occupier.

Visitors

KEY DEFINITION: Visitor

Any person who comes onto premises with either the express or implied permission of the occupier will be a visitor.

KEY STATUTE

Occupiers' Liability Act 1957, s. 2

Section 2 requires occupiers of premises to take:

> such care as in all the circumstances of the case is reasonable to see that the visitor will be reasonably safe in using the premises for the purposes for which he is invited or permitted by the occupier to be there.

This standard of care is similar to the standard required in the tort of negligence. But remember that the standard of care demanded varies with all the circumstances, so a higher standard is owed to children.

Notices that warn of danger might mean that the occupier is not liable, but only if they enable the lawful visitor to be reasonably safe in visiting the premises. Notices that try to restrict liability for injury to lawful visitors will be subject to the Unfair Contract Terms Act 1977.

REVISION NOTE

Earlier in this chapter we saw that s. 2(1) of that Act provides that liability in respect of death or personal injury caused by negligence can never be excluded. We also saw that s. 2(2) provides that liability for damage other than death or personal injury can be excluded, but only by a term or notice which is reasonable.

Damages can be claimed only in respect of injuries or losses which were of a reasonably foreseeable type. *Volenti non fit injuria* can be a complete defence and contributory negligence can reduce the amount of damages awarded.

Non-lawful visitors

People who enter premises other than as visitors do so as non-visitors, generally referred to as trespassers.

KEY STATUTE

Occupiers' Liability Act 1984, s. 1(3)

Section 1(3) of the OLA 1984 extends a statutory duty of protection to trespassers. The occupier owes the duty to take such care as is reasonable to see that the trespasser is not injured. The duty arises if three conditions are met:

1. the occupier knows or ought to know that a danger exists;
2. the occupier knows or ought to know that the trespasser is in the vicinity of the danger; and
3. the risk is one against which the occupier could, in all the circumstances of the case, reasonably be expected to offer the trespasser some protection.

Liability under the Occupiers' Liability Act 1984 can arise only for personal injuries. The Unfair Contract Terms Act 1977 does not apply to the duty of care created by the 1984 Act.

Consumer Protection Act 1987, Part I

The CPA 1987, Part 1 allows a claimant who is injured by an unsafe product to sue the manufacturer of the product, and possibly others, without having to prove negligence. Liability under the Act is strict.

Who can be liable?

The CPA 1987 places liability on the **producer of a product**.

KEY DEFINITION: Producer of a product

Sections 1 and 2 of the CPA 1987 define the producer of a product as including:

- the manufacturer of the product;
- the extractor of raw materials;
- industrial processors of agricultural produce;
- 'own branders' who add their label to products which they did not produce;
- anyone who imports the product into the EU.

If more than one of these people are liable the injured person can sue any or all of them.

Defective products

A producer of a product is liable only if a defective product causes injury. However, you must remember that here 'defective' does not have its usual meaning.

KEY STATUTE

Consumer Protection Act 1987, s. 3

Section 3 says that products can be regarded as defective if their *safety* 'is not such as persons generally are entitled to expect'.

The court will consider all the circumstances when deciding whether or not the objective standard which the Act requires has been breached. The Act does, however, mention a number of factors to be considered, including the following:

- the way in which the product was marketed;
- instructions and warnings issued with the product;
- what might reasonably be expected to be done with the product;
- the time at which the product was supplied.

Damage suffered

Section 5 of the CPA 1987 allows a claimant to claim damages for death or any personal injury.

Damage to non-business property is claimable, but only if it causes an individual to suffer a loss of more than £275. The loss may be made up of damage to several items.

Damage to the product itself is not recoverable. Nor is damage to other products supplied with the product.

Compensation for injury, death and damage to goods must be claimed within three years of the loss becoming apparent. In addition, there is an absolute time limit of ten years after the date when the product was supplied.

Defences

Under the CPA 1987 liability is strict and this means that the claimant does not need to prove fault. Nor can liability be excluded by any contract term or notice. Contributory negligence might reduce the amount of damages payable. In addition, the Act sets out the following defences:

Figure 5.1

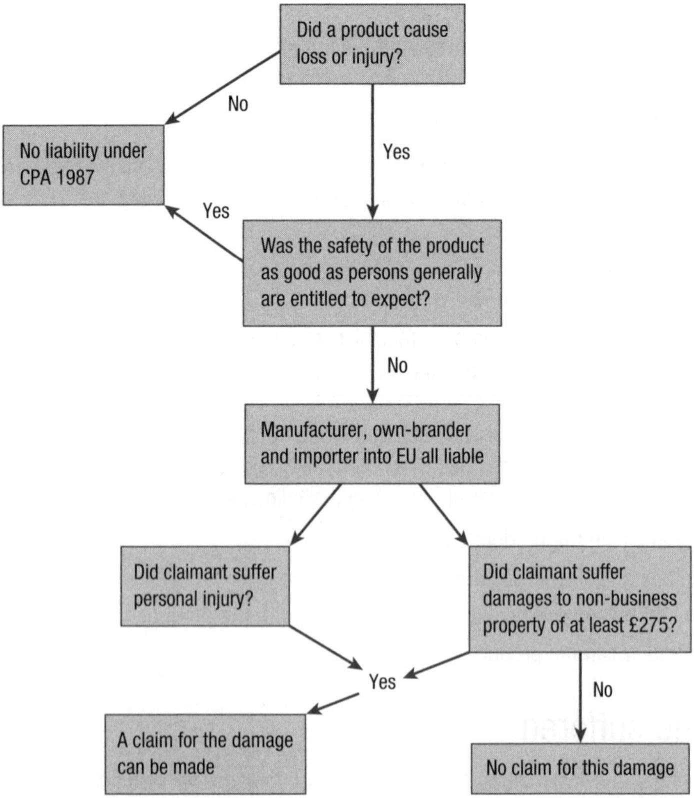

- The defect was caused by complying with EC or UK legislation.
- The product was not supplied or manufactured in the course of a business.
- The defect in the product did not exist when the product was put onto the market.
- A supplier of a component will have a defence if the unsafety arose because the manufacturer of the finished product misused the component.
- The development risks defence is available to a producer if he can show that when he produced it the state of scientific and technical knowledge was '*not such that a producer of products of the same description as the product in question might be expected to have discovered it*'.

Figure 5.1 gives an overview of the CPA 1987, Part 1.

Private nuisance

KEY DEFINITION: Private nuisance

Private nuisance is a substantial, unreasonable interference with a claimant's land or with a claimant's use or enjoyment of land.

Only an owner of land or a person with a right to be in possession of land, such as a tenant, can sue.

Any person who has control of premises where the nuisance is caused can be liable. So too can an occupier of premises who gives authority for the nuisance to be committed.

In order to succeed in an action for nuisance, the claimant must prove that the nuisance has caused some damage, either to the land itself or to the use and enjoyment of the land.

Foreseeability

The Wagon Mound test is applicable (see p. 83). So a defendant will not be liable in nuisance unless the damage suffered was of a type which the defendant could reasonably foresee. However, as long as the type of damage was reasonably foreseeable even a defendant who had taken all reasonable care could be liable. So liability is strict but not absolute.

Remedies

Damages

Damages will be quantified using the same principles as apply when quantifying damages for negligence (see p. 84). The defendant must take reasonable steps to mitigate any loss and so will not be able to claim damages for losses which could have been mitigated by taking reasonable steps.

Injunction

An injunction is generally the most sought-after remedy for private nuisance.

Abatement

Abatement allows a claimant to remove the nuisance if this can be done without entering onto the defendant's land. The remedy is available only in an emergency or only if it is inappropriate to bring legal proceedings.

Defences

Statutory authority

A defendant will not be liable for a nuisance which was necessarily committed in order to comply with a statute.

Prescription

Prescription is a property right which can allow a person to continue committing what would otherwise be a nuisance. The right is acquired by continuously doing the act which causes the nuisance for 20 years. However, the act must be committed without force, openly and without permission and must have amounted to a nuisance for the whole 20 years.

Consent of claimant

It is a complete defence that the claimant consented to the nuisance being committed. (The defence of consent was considered in relation to negligence. See *volenti non fit injuria* earlier in the chapter [on p. 84].)

Contributory negligence

This might be a defence where the nuisance was committed by negligent conduct.

Public nuisance

Public nuisance is both a crime and a tort. It is committed by any act or omission which endangers the health, property or comfort of the public, or which prevents the public from exercising rights which all citizens enjoy. In order to be able to bring an action the claimant must show that the nuisance has caused more damage to him or her than to the public generally. Only a person who has some control over the nuisance can be liable for public nuisance. Many actions for public nuisance concern obstructing a highway.

Damages or an injunction are available as remedies. Statutory authority, consent and contributory negligence are available as defences.

The rule in *Rylands* v. *Fletcher*

The rule in *Rylands* v. *Fletcher* is the name given to a tort of strict liability. In the case itself (1866) the rule was explained by Blackburn J:

> The person who for his own purposes brings on his lands and collects and keeps there anything likely to do mischief if it escapes, must bring it at his peril, and if he does not do so, is . . . answerable for all the damage which is the natural consequence of its escape.

The requirements of the tort are:

- the defendant must either bring something onto his or her land or let it accumulate there;
- this must be a non-natural use of the land;
- the thing must be likely to do mischief if it escapes;
- the thing must escape and cause damage.

Remedies

The remedy for this tort is damages and the position as regards damages is the same as the position for private nuisance, considered earlier in this chapter.

Statutory authority and contributory negligence are available as defences. Both of these were considered earlier in this chapter, in relation to the tort of nuisance. **Act of God** and consent of the claimant are additional defences.

Trespass to land

Trespass to land is committed by a direct, unauthorised invasion of another person's land. Only a person in possession of land can sue. The tort can be committed intentionally or negligently.

Defences and remedies

Statutory authority, considered above in relation to private nuisance, is a defence. It is also a defence that permission to enter has been expressly or impliedly granted. Damages or an injunction are available as remedies.

REVISION NOTE

You should remember that:

- trespass to land involves a direct physical invasion of land;
- private nuisance is not a direct physical invasion but an unreasonable interference with the use and enjoyment of land;
- public nuisance is an act or omission which endangers the public or prevents the public from exercising rights; and
- the rule in *Rylands* v. *Fletcher* arises when any non-natural thing brought onto the land (or allowed to accumulate there) causes mischief when it escapes.

Trespass to the person

There are three torts of trespass to the person: battery, assault and false imprisonment.

1. Battery is committed by any direct and intentional physical contact with the claimant's body without the claimant's consent.
2. Assault is committed by any act which directly and intentionally causes the claimant to reasonably fear that he or she is immediately about to suffer battery.
3. False imprisonment is committed by directly and intentionally depriving the claimant of his or her liberty.

Defences to trespass to the person

Consent and statutory authority are available as defences. Contributory negligence is not a defence.

Trespass to goods

The tort of *conversion* is the main form of trespass to goods. It is committed if the defendant deals with goods in a manner which is inconsistent with the right of another person to possess the goods. Conversion can be committed by a person who does not know that he or she is denying somebody else the right to possess the goods. However, a defendant cannot be liable in conversion unless he or she intentionally intended to deal with the goods.

Vicarious liability

Employers are vicariously liable for torts committed by their employees during the course of their employment. In Chapter 9, employees and independent contractors are distinguished. Here we need to consider the circumstances in which employees are acting in the course of their employment. The courts have devised the following tests:

- An employee will be acting in the course of employment when doing what he or she was expressly or impliedly authorised to do.
- If an employee is authorised to do an act properly then the employer will be liable if the employee performs the act negligently.
- If an employee commits a tort while doing an act which is designed to help the employer then the employer will be liable.
- If an employee does something entirely for his own benefit he is said to be 'on a frolic of his own', and the employer will not be liable.

The tort of breach of statutory duty

In some cases a statute may impose duties without mentioning civil remedies. In such a situation a person who has suffered harm as a result of a breach of the statutory duty might try to sue in tort. To succeed it must be shown that Parliament intended liability in tort to ensue, despite its not having mentioned such liability in the statute.

It is essential that the legislation in question imposes an obligation upon the defendant. The claimant must also show that he or she was within a class which was intended to benefit from the statute, and that the statute indicates that Parliament intended to give a right to sue if the statute was breached.

Putting it all together

Answer guidelines

See the problem question at the start of the chapter.

Approaching the question

Seema might be able to sue Ted in the tort of negligence. Anjana might be able to sue the producer of the microwave under the Consumer Protection Act 1987, Part 1. ▶

Important points to include

- Have you considered all of the requirements of the tort of negligence, in respect of both Seema and her employer? (Duty of care owed, duty breached, causation and remoteness.)
- Have you considered any possible defences?
- Have you considered how damages might be assessed?
- Have you followed your way through all the requirements of the CPA 1987, Part 1, paying attention to matters such as who the 'producer' of the microwave might be, whether the microwave was defective and whether damages can be claimed for all of Anjana's loss?

✓ Make your answer stand out

Plan your answer logically. Deal thoroughly with matters such as foreseeability and whether a duty is owed in respect of pure economic loss.

READ TO IMPRESS

Lord Hoffmann (2005) Causation, 121 LQR 59

Stapleton, J. (1998) The Gist of Negligence, 104 LQR 213

Stauch, M. (2001) Risk and Remoteness of Damage in Negligence, 64 MLR 191

Williams, G. (1951) The Aims of the Law of Tort, CLP 137

Witting, C. (2001) Distinguishing between Property Damage and Pure Economic Loss: A Personality Thesis, 21(3) LS 481–514

www.pearsoned.co.uk/lawexpress

Go online to access more revision support including quizzes to test your knowledge, sample questions with answer guidelines, podcasts you can download, and more!

6 Companies 1: Formation and personnel

Revision checklist

Essential points you should know:

- [ ] The characteristics of a company
- [ ] The way in which a company is formed
- [ ] The rules relating to a company name
- [ ] The rules relating to company directors
- [ ] The roles of the company secretary and the auditor

Topic map

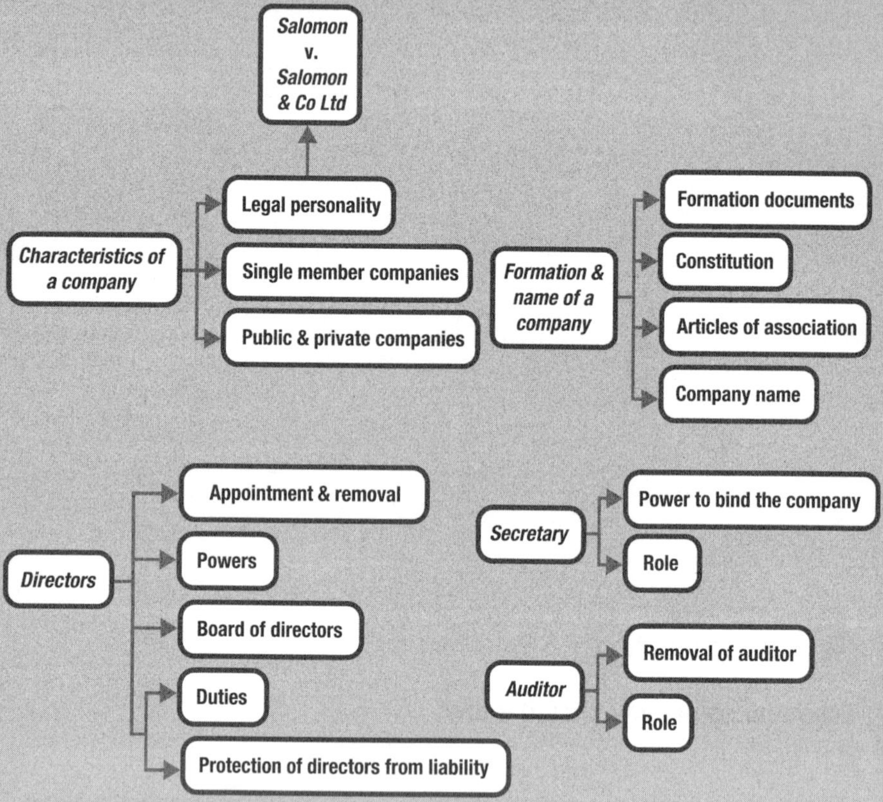

A printable version of this topic map is available from **www.pearsoned.co.uk/lawexpress**

Introduction

This chapter sets out the law relating to directors of companies, a subject which features in almost all problem questions on company law.

In addition, the chapter considers the nature of a company, how a company is formed, the company secretary and the auditor.

ASSESSMENT ADVICE

Essay questions

Essay questions are most likely to concern the duties of directors and the consequences of breach of such duties. Make sure that you can explain the new statutory duties and give examples of how they might be breached.

Problem questions

Problem questions generally involve duties of directors, the powers of the directors and the secretary to bind the company and removal of a director from office. If you can take a statute book into the exam with you, do not copy out the relevant sections of the Companies Act 2006. Instead, make sure that you *apply* the relevant sections to the problem.

Sample question

Could you answer this question? Below is a typical problem question that could arise on this topic. Guidelines on answering the question are included at the end of this chapter, while a sample essay question and guidance on tackling it can be found on the companion website.

PROBLEM QUESTION

A Ltd is a company which sells and fits double-glazing. David has never been appointed as managing director of A Ltd, but the other four directors have always allowed him to act as managing director. David ordered a new sports car in the company name. The car was bought from Beta Cars Ltd for £43,000. David intended to use this car as his personal company car and subsequently sold the existing company car, worth £8,000, to his brother for £2,000. The other directors are refusing to be bound by the contract to buy the sports car on two grounds. First, that David had no ▶

authority to buy the car on behalf of the company. Second, that the contract was outside the company's objects as stated in the objects clause.

The directors now want to remove David as a director, even though the company articles state that he is to be a director for life. They also wish to claim damages from David in the event that the company suffers a loss as a result of either of the two contracts which David made.

Advise the company of its legal position.

Companies Act 2006

The Companies Act 2006, which has replaced the 1985 Companies Act, has four main objectives:

1. to enhance shareholder engagement and to foster a long-term approach to investment;
2. to adopt a 'Think Small First' approach and to ensure that companies are better regulated;
3. to make it easier to create and run a company;
4. to provide flexibility for the future.

The 'Think Small First' approach means that the Act is often structured in such a way that it makes rules for small companies, and then adds more rules for plcs and then still more rules for quoted companies.

Legal personality

A company has a legal identity of its own, which is quite separate from the legal identity of its owners. Legally, a company is a person.

KEY CASE

***Salomon* v. *Salomon and Co Ltd* [1897] AC 22 (HL)**

Concerning: the legal personality of a company

Facts

Salomon owned all but six of a company's 20,000 registered shares. The company went into liquidation, owing large sums to creditors. These creditors said that Salomon should pay the company's debts.

Legal principle

The shareholders of a company are not the company. A company is a legal person. So Salomon had no obligation to pay the company's debts.

The legal personality of a company has the following consequences:

- Members of a limited company have limited liability for the debts of the company. Almost all companies are limited companies (this book does not consider unlimited companies).
- A company has 'perpetual succession' and so continues in existence until it is wound up.
- A company can own property, and this property will continue to be owned by the company regardless of who owns the shares in the company.
- A company has the power to make contracts, and can sue and be sued on these contracts.
- Companies can be guilty of crimes.

KEY STATUTE

Corporate Manslaughter and Corporate Homicide Act 2007

The CMCHA 2007 has created a new offence of corporate manslaughter which can be committed by companies and by other incorporated bodies, such as LLPs. (LLPs are considered in Chapter 8.) The Director of Public Prosecutions must consent to a prosecution being brought. A company will be guilty of corporate manslaughter if the way in which its activities are managed and organised:

- causes a person's death, and
- amounts to a gross breach of a relevant duty of care owed by the organisation to the deceased.

Many criminal offences committed by companies are offences of strict liability. If *mens rea* is required, the courts can regard the controllers of the company as the minds of the company.

The corporate veil

We have seen that a company has a legal identity of its own. The company's shareholders (members) are said be protected by the 'veil of incorporation'. This image is used because a veil shields the face of the person behind it, and the 'veil of incorporation' shields the members from liability for the company's debts and wrongs. However, the veil can be lifted, and company members can be made personally liable, in very limited circumstances where a person deliberately evades an existing legal obligation, liability or restriction by means of a company under his or her control.

Public companies	Private companies
Name must end with the words 'Public Limited Company' or 'plc'	Name must end with 'Limited' or 'Ltd' (unless the company is unlimited)
Must have £50,000 allotted share capital, one quarter of which must be paid up	No minimum share capital
Shares can be listed on stock exchange (no requirement that they should be listed)	Shares cannot be listed on stock exchange, or advertised for sale
Must have at least two directors	Need have only one director
Shares allotted by the company must be paid for in cash (or qualified auditor must value assets given as payment)	Shares can be given away by the company
Must have a company secretary, who must be suitably qualified	No need to have a company secretary – if there is one, does not need to be qualified
Must hold AGM every calendar year	No AGM, or any other meeting of members, unless positive decision taken to hold one
Cannot pass written resolutions	Can pass written resolutions

Public and private companies

Limited companies can be either public companies or private companies. The table above shows the differences between the two.

Single member companies

The 2006 Act allows both private and public companies to have only one member. New companies can be created with only one member or an existing company can allow its membership to fall to one.

Forming a new company

A new company is created by promoters, who must register the company under the Companies Act 2006. The 2006 Act has changed the process of registering a company. Under the new Act, a company is formed by one or more persons sending the following to the Registrar of Companies:

- a memorandum of association;
- an application for registration, along with certain documents required by the Act;
- a statement of compliance; and
- a £20 fee.

New-style memorandum of association

The **new-style memorandum of association** is quite different from the old-style memorandum.

KEY DEFINITION: New-style memorandum of association

A new-style memorandum of association merely states that the subscribers, the people who sign it, wish to form a company under the 2006 Act and that they agree to become members of the company by taking at least one share each.

A new-style memorandum will not be capable of being changed later. It gives a 'historical snapshot' of the company members on formation of the company. An old-style memorandum was of much more significance. Under the 2006 Act the significant contents of an existing company's old-style memorandum are automatically transferred to the company's articles of association. The articles of association are considered later in this chapter (see p. 103).

The application for registration

We have seen that an application for registration must be sent to the Registrar along with a new-style memorandum. The application for registration must state:

- the company's proposed name;
- whether the company's registered office is to be situated in England and Wales (or in Wales), in Scotland or in Northern Ireland;
- whether the liability of the members of the company is to be limited, and if so whether it is to be limited by shares or guarantee;
- whether the company is to be a public company or a private company;
- a statement of share capital and initial shareholdings;
- a statement of the intended address of the company's registered office; and
- a statement of any proposed articles of association, to the extent that model articles are not being used.

The statement of *capital and initial shareholdings* is required to state the following:

- the total number of shares to be taken on formation by the subscribers to the memorandum;
- the total nominal value of those shares;
- the amount to be paid up and the amount (if any) to be unpaid on each share.

The statement of *proposed officers* must give the names and addresses and details of the first directors and the first company secretary (if the company is to have a company secretary).

The Registrar can accept the **statement of compliance** as evidence that the requirements of the Act have been complied with and will then issue a certificate of incorporation. The company then exists and is able to trade.

KEY DEFINITION: Statement of compliance

The statement of compliance states that the Act's requirements as to registration have been complied with.

Constitution of a company

Section 17 of the 2006 Act provides that a company's constitution is made up of:

- the company's articles of association;
- special resolutions; and
- unanimous agreements of the members which would have needed to have been passed as special resolutions.

Legal effect of the constitution

KEY STATUTE

Companies Act 2006, s. 33(1)

Section 33(1) of the Act provides that:

> The provisions of a company's constitution bind the company and its members to the same extent as if they were covenants on the part of each member to observe those provisions.
>
> So the constitution has the legal effect of making a contract between each member and the company, and a contract between every member and every other member. However, this is true only in relation to matters concerning membership of the company.

Resolutions which form part of the constitution must be sent to the Registrar within 15 days of their being passed. An up-to-date copy of the constitutional documents must be sent to any member who requests one.

Articles of association

The articles of association are the rules of the company. A company must have articles of association and these must be contained in a single document which is divided into consecutively numbered paragraphs.

Different sets of model articles, suitable for different types of companies, have been drawn up. These articles will *apply by default* when a company is formed under the 2006 Act, unless other articles are registered. Even if other articles are registered, the model articles will still apply to the extent that they are not excluded or modified by the articles which are registered.

Companies already in existence before the 2006 Act came into force will not be governed by the new model articles, unless they choose to adopt them. Many companies formed before the 2006 Act came into force use a different set of model articles, known as Table A model articles.

KEY STATUTE

Companies Act 2006, s. 28(1)

Section 28(1) provides that matters which used to be contained in an old-style memorandum of association, before the commencement of the 2006 Act, are to be treated as provisions of the company's articles from the time when the Act came into force. The most important matter which is transferred to the articles is the 'objects clause', the effect of which is considered later (see p. 109).

Amendment of articles

A company's articles may generally be amended by special resolution. Such a resolution is passed only if at least 75% of company members who vote on it vote in favour of it. However, some articles may be **entrenched articles of association**.

KEY DEFINITION: Entrenched articles of association

Entrenched articles of association are articles that can be amended or repealed only if conditions are met, or procedures complied with, which are more restrictive than those applicable in the case of a special resolution.

The Act does not specify what these conditions might be. However, since a special resolution requires a 75% majority of those voting on it, the procedures might require procedures such as a unanimous vote or a vote passed by a 90% majority of all company members. Provision for entrenchment can be made only in the company's articles when the company is formed, or by an amendment of the articles agreed to by all the members of the company.

It is not possible to make entrenched articles unalterable.

Whenever a company's articles are amended, the company must send the Registrar a copy of the amended articles within 15 days of the amendment taking effect.

✓ Make your answer stand out

Why should it be possible to have entrenched articles? If 75% of members want to change an article should they not always be able to pass a special resolution to do so? What problems might then be caused to members who hold 25% or less of the company's shares? Would the rules on protection of the minority, set out in the following chapter (on pp. 126–129) not provide the minority with enough protection?

Company name

The name of a company is important because it is the means by which the company, a legal person, can be identified. The following names are prohibited:

- names which are offensive;
- names which suggest a connection with government or a local authority;
- names which have already been registered by another company;
- names which would falsely indicate a connection with a charitable organisation, or that the company is a bank or a building society.

The 2006 Act allows letters, signs, punctuation marks and symbols to be used in a company name, as long as they comply with an approved list made by the Secretary of State.

The name of a public company must end with the words 'public limited company' or the abbreviation 'plc'. The name of a private limited company must end with the word 'limited' or the abbreviation 'Ltd'. If the company is registered in Wales the Welsh equivalents of these words and abbreviations may be used instead.

Objection to a company name

It is possible to object to a company name.

KEY STATUTE

Companies Act 2006, s. 69

Section 69 allows any person to object to a company's registered name on one of two grounds:

(a) that it is the same as a name associated with the applicant in which the applicant has goodwill, or

(b) that it is sufficiently similar to such a name that its use in the United Kingdom would be likely to mislead by suggesting a connection between the company and the applicant.

Complaints are made to a *company names adjudicator* who can order a company to change its name.

Change of name

A company may change its name:

- by **special resolution**; or
- by an **ordinary resolution** following a direction from the Secretary of State or a decision from the company names adjudicator; or
- by other means provided for by the company's articles.

KEY DEFINITION: Ordinary and special resolutions

Both ordinary and special resolutions are passed by the members of the company. An *ordinary resolution* is passed if more than 50% of members who vote cast their votes in favour of the resolution. A *special resolution* is passed only if at least 75% of members who vote cast their votes in favour of it. Resolutions are considered in more detail in the following chapter (see pp. 121–4).

Where a name is changed by special resolution, the company must give notice to the Registrar. The same prohibitions will apply to a change of name as applied to the use of a name on formation of a company. When a name is successfully changed, the Registrar must issue a new certificate of incorporation.

Publication of name and address

All companies must publish their names legibly and conspicuously:

- outside the registered office and all places of business;
- on all letters, invoices, notices, cheques, orders for goods and receipts;
- on the company seal, if it has a seal.

These rules ensure that people dealing with a company know that they are dealing with a company.

Directors

A company is managed by its board of directors and by others to whom the board delegates authority.

A private company must have at least one director. A public company must have at least two. All companies must have at least one director who is a *natural person* (not another company or an LLP).

Appointment of directors

When a company is formed the statement of proposed officers names the first directors of the company. Subsequent directors are appointed by an ordinary resolution of the members unless the company's articles provide otherwise.

No person under 16 years of age can be appointed a director. There is no maximum age for directors.

Retirement and removal of directors

A director may resign at any time, and the company is obliged to accept the resignation.

KEY STATUTE

Companies Act 2006, s. 168(1)

No matter what a company's articles might say, and no matter what might have been agreed between the director and the company, s. 168(1) provides that a director can always be removed by an ordinary resolution of which the company has been given special (28 days') notice, as long as the resolution is passed at a meeting of the company members.

You should remember that s. 168(1) is necessary only where the company's articles do not allow a director to be removed by ordinary resolution. You should also remember that a written resolution cannot be used to remove a director under s. 168(1), because the director is entitled to be heard at the meeting.

If a company receives special notice of a resolution to remove a director under s. 168(1), s. 169(1) provides that the company must immediately send a copy of the notice to the director concerned. Even if he or she is not a member of the company, the director whose dismissal is proposed has a right to speak at the meeting (s. 169(2)). Section 169(3) allows the director also to make written representations, of a reasonable length, to the members. If the company receives these representations in time, it must send them out to members along with notice of the meeting. If the representations are not received in time, the director has the right to require them to be read out at the meeting (as well as the right to be heard orally).

Disqualification of directors

Section 11 of the Company Directors Disqualification Act 1986 makes it a criminal offence of strict liability for an undischarged bankrupt to be concerned in the management of a company.

Additionally, a person who is the subject of a **disqualification order** may not take part in the management of a company or promote a company.

KEY DEFINITION: Disqualification order

A disqualification order is a court order which prevents a person from being a director, or from being concerned in the management of a company, without approval from the court.

A person who ignores such an order commits a criminal offence and can be made personally liable for all debts and liabilities incurred while acting in contravention.

A disqualification order may be made under CDDA 1986 on a number of grounds. Generally, these involve fraud, dishonesty or persistent failure to comply with the requirements of the Companies Act.

Register of directors

Every company must keep a register of its directors, giving the following information about each director who is an individual:

- name and any former name;
- a service address;
- the country in which he or she is usually resident;
- nationality;
- business occupation (if any); and
- date of birth.

The service address is an address at which documents may be effectively served on that person. To ensure privacy, it can be stated to be 'The company's registered office'.

The register of directors must be kept available for inspection at the company's registered office or at a place specified in Regulations made by the Secretary of State. The members of the company are entitled to inspect it free of charge. Non-members are entitled to inspect it upon payment of a small fee.

Protection from disclosure of residential address

A director's residential address is 'protected information', even after the director has left the company. The company must not use or disclose this protected information, unless it does so for one of three purposes:

1. communicating with the director in question; or
2. sending required particulars to the Registrar of Companies; or
3. under a court order.

The board of directors

When the directors act collectively they act as the board of directors. They must act as a board unless they have delegated their powers. Meetings of the board of directors are known as *board meetings*. You should remember that a board meeting is quite different from a general meeting of the company. All company members are entitled to attend a general meeting.

A company's articles may allow for the existence of a *managing director* who acts as chief executive officer in charge of the day-to-day administration of the company. The board of directors can delegate some or all of their powers to such a managing director.

If a company gives the impression that a person has been appointed managing director, then a third party can take it that the person had the powers of a managing director. This is known as *holding out*. The company is said to have held out that the person was managing director and is therefore estopped from denying this. The company will be estopped if three conditions are satisfied:

1. there must have been a representation that the person was managing director of the company;
2. this representation must have been made by the company or by someone with authority to make it on the company's behalf; and
3. the other contracting party must have relied on the representation.

Remuneration of directors

Directors will only be entitled to be paid fees for their services if the constitution of the company provides for payment, or if the payment is approved by the members. Payments to directors do not depend upon the company having made a profit.

Directors' powers

The powers of the directors will be contained in the company's articles of association. So the balance of power between the members and the directors varies from company to company. You should remember that in many small companies the members and the directors are the same people.

Generally, articles would provide that the directors are responsible for the management of the company's business, for which purpose they may exercise all the powers of the company.

Many articles would also provide that the members could pass a special resolution requiring the directors either to do or not to do a certain thing.

The members of a company can *ratify* acts committed by directors in excess of their authority. If this is done the authority which was lacking is supplied later and the act in question is then adopted as an act of the company as if the necessary authority had always existed. An ordinary resolution is needed, unless the act was outside the company's objects, in which case a special resolution is needed.

Effect of an objects clause

Before the 2006 Act came into force all companies had to have an **objects clause**.

KEY DEFINITION: Objects clause

An objects clause is a clause, required to be contained in an old-style memorandum of association, which sets out the 'objects' of the company. That is to say, it sets out the types of contract which the company could validly make.

However, even before the 2006 Act came into force a company could state that its objects were to carry on business as a general commercial company. This made the objects clause ineffective because it meant that the company could carry on any trade or business whatsoever.

Earlier in this chapter, we saw that s. 28(1) has transferred matters which were contained in a company's old-style memorandum into the company's articles. So now any objects clause will be in a company's articles.

KEY STATUTE

Companies Act 2006, s. 31

Unless a company's articles specifically restrict the objects of the company, its objects are unrestricted.

This important section allows a company not to have an objects clause at all. However, you should remember that most companies will have an objects clause, either because they choose to have one or because an objects clause in their old-style memorandum has been transferred to the company's articles.

If a company acts for a purpose outside the company's objects clause the contract is said to be *ultra vires* (beyond the powers). If this contract causes loss to the company, any director who made the contract is personally liable to reimburse the company for the money lost. The members can excuse the director from making this payment, but a special resolution is needed to do this. In addition, another special resolution must be passed, ratifying the *ultra vires* transaction.

It used to be the case, before 1972, that if a company made a contract which was outside its objects clause the contract was void. This is no longer the case.

KEY STATUTE

Companies Act 2006, s. 39(1) and 40(1)

39(1) The validity of an act done by a company shall not be called into question on the ground of lack of capacity by reason of anything in the company's constitution.

40(1) In favour of a person dealing with a company in good faith, the power of the directors to bind the company, or authorise others to do so, is deemed to be free of any limitation under the company's constitution.

A person dealing with the company is deemed to have acted in good faith unless the contrary is proved.

So a contract cannot now be made void because it is *ultra vires*. However, company members can get an injunction to prevent the making of an *ultra vires* contract which has not yet been made.

Section 41 provides that an *ultra vires* transaction entered into between the company and the directors of the company is voidable by the company, despite s. 40. The directors at fault have to account to the company for any gain they have made from the contract and also have to indemnify the company for any loss it has suffered.

REVISION NOTE

The meaning of voidable, and the quite different meaning of void, were explained in Chapter 3 (on p. 55). If you have forgotten what voidable means, look again at that explanation.

Directors' duties

The 2006 Act has partially codified the law relating to directors' duties. The duties set out in ss. 171–177 are called *general duties*. They are owed by a director to the company (s. 170(1)).

The seven general statutory duties are as follows.

Section	Duty
s. 171	To act within powers
s. 172	To promote the success of the company
s. 173	To exercise independent judgement
s. 174	To exercise reasonable care, skill and diligence
s. 175	To avoid conflicts of interest
s. 176	Not to accept benefits from third parties
s. 177	To declare an interest in a proposed transaction or arrangement

These general directors' duties give rise to civil liability and will generally be enforceable only by the company, i.e. by the board of directors or by the members in general meeting. However, a member might be able to bring a statutory *derivative claim* (see pp. 126–7) on behalf of the company.

✎ EXAM TIP

If a problem question concerns directors' duties, do not forget to consider all of the duties which might have been breached. Do not regard the question as answered just because one duty has been breached.

Declaration of interest in existing transaction or arrangement

Section 182 sets out a further duty of a director to declare any interest in an existing transaction with a company. This duty is not regarded as one of the general duties, as it imposes criminal liability and breach of it has no civil consequences.

Transactions with directors requiring approval of members

The following four types of transaction between a director and the company must be approved by the members:

1. contracts which employ the directors for more than five years;
2. substantial property transactions;

3. loans to directors; and
4. payments of over £200 for loss of office.

Protection of directors from liability

The company's constitution might contain provisions which try to protect directors from liability, or the members might ratify wrongful acts of directors.

KEY STATUTE

Companies Act 2006, s. 232(1)

Section 232(1) provides that any provision that purports to exempt a director of a company (to any extent) from any liability that would otherwise attach to him in connection with any negligence, default, breach of duty or breach of trust in relation to the company is void. This does not, however, prevent the members from passing a resolution ratifying the negligent conduct of a director.

Despite s. 232(1), s. 232(4) allows a director to have an interest in a transaction which conflicts with the interests of the company as long as the articles permit this and the interest has been disclosed to the directors. Section 175(4–6) allows what would otherwise be a conflict of interest if the directors have properly authorised the act in line with the company's constitution. However, the director in question does not count towards the **quorum** of the meeting and cannot vote in favour of authorisation.

KEY DEFINITION: Quorum

A quorum is the minimum number of people required to be present at a meeting before the meeting can validly take place.

Ratification of acts giving rise to liability

Section 239 retains the common law right of the members to pass a resolution saying that the company is ratifying conduct by a director amounting to negligence, default, or breach of duty of trust in relation to the company. An ordinary resolution will be enough unless the articles require more. However, the common law rule that a fraudulent act cannot be ratified is retained by the 2006 Act.

Relief from the court

Section 1157 allows the court to excuse a director (or company secretary or auditor) in breach of his or her duty from liability if the director 'acted honestly and reasonably and ought fairly to be excused'.

Company secretary

A company secretary does not manage the company but performs administrative tasks on behalf of the company. Private companies no longer need to have a company secretary but every plc must have one. The directors must ensure that the secretary of a plc is a *suitably qualified person*. This means that the secretary must either:

- hold professionally recognised qualifications, as an accountant or a UK qualified lawyer; or
- have been a secretary of a public company for three of the past five years; or
- appear to the directors to be capable of discharging the duties and functions of a company secretary, by virtue of holding or having held any other position, or being a member of any other body.

The articles of a company usually provide that the company secretary is appointed, and can be removed, by the directors.

The company secretary is not a manager of the company and is not concerned in carrying on the business of the company.

The company secretary has a limited power to bind the company, but only as regards the types of administrative contract which a company secretary could be expected to make. Outsiders acting in good faith can take it that the company secretary can make these types of administrative contract. This is because the secretary has been *held out* by the company as having the authority to make them.

REVISION NOTE

The requirements of holding out were considered earlier in this chapter, in relation to a person being held out as managing director (see p. 108).

KEY CASE

***Panorama Developments (Guildford) Ltd* v. *Fidelis Furnishing Fabrics Ltd* [1971] 3 All ER 16 (CA)**

Concerning: the type of contract which a company secretary can make

Facts

A company secretary hired cars in the company name. It appeared to the hirers that the cars were being used to meet the company's customers. In fact the secretary was using the cars for his own purposes. The hirers sued the company for the hire charges and the company was held liable to pay them. ▶

Legal principle

By appointing a person company secretary the company holds that person out as having authority to make administrative contracts.

Lord Denning MR said:

> A company secretary . . . is certainly entitled to sign contracts connected with the administrative side of the company's affairs, such as employing staff, and ordering cars, and so forth.

! Don't be tempted to . . .

You should not think that the appointment of a person as company secretary always makes the same representation as to that person's power to bind the company. When a representation is made by conduct, as happens when a person is appointed company secretary, it can be very difficult to say exactly what has been represented. The answer can be found only by considering all of the circumstances surrounding the representation. For example, would it be represented that the company secretary of a very small company could make the same contracts as the secretary of a very large company?

The auditor

The auditor is not the company accountant, but a different accountant who keeps an eye on the company's accounts and accounting procedures. The auditor is appointed by the members of the company and reports to the members.

The need to have an auditor

Small *private* companies are exempt from having to have their accounts audited. In this context a company is regarded as small in a particular year if:

- the company's annual turnover is £5.6m or less; and
- the total assets of the company are £2.8m or less.

The auditor is neither a manager nor an employee of the company. Unlike the directors and the secretary, the auditor is an independent contractor.

REVISION NOTE

In Chapter 9 (on pp. 152–3) the difference between working as an employee and working as an independent contractor is considered.

Auditors must be appointed for each financial year of the company, unless the directors reasonably resolve otherwise on the ground that audited accounts are unlikely to be required.

Auditors' liability

Auditors can be liable to the company either for breach of contract or in negligence.

Section 532 provides that any agreement exempting an auditor from liability is void. Despite this, s. 534 allows for *liability limitation* agreements between companies and their auditors. Such an agreement can relate to only one financial year and must be authorised by the company members passing a resolution at a company meeting. An ordinary resolution will be enough unless the company's articles require a higher threshold.

Section 537(1) limits the effect of a liability limitation agreement by providing that the auditor's liability cannot be limited to less than such amount as is fair and reasonable in all the circumstances. Particular regard should be had to:

- the auditor's responsibilities;
- the nature and purpose of the auditor's contractual obligations to the company; and
- the professional standards expected of him or her.

Putting it all together

Answer guidelines

See the problem question at the start of the chapter.

Approaching the question

You will need to consider the following matters.

- Is the company bound by the contract to buy the company car even though David had never been appointed managing director?
- Could the fact that the purchase of the car was outside the objects clause invalidate the contract?
- Did David breach any general duties in either purchasing the sports car or selling the old car?

Could David be removed as a director? If so, what steps would need to be taken? ▶

Important points to include

- You should explain the effect of David being held out as the managing director.
- You should apply CA 2006 ss. 39(1) and 40(1) to the contract under which David bought the car.
- Consider each of the statutory duties in turn, as regards both the car which David bought and the car which he sold.
- Apply CA 2006 s. 168(1) when considering whether or not the other directors can remove David as a director.

✓ Make your answer stand out

Apply the law thoughtfully. For example, the question does not tell you whether or not Beta Cars Ltd were aware that David had in the past been allowed to act as if he was managing director. When considering holding out you should therefore consider the position both if Beta Cars Ltd were aware of this and if they were not. Also, do not consider just one general duty which might have been breached. Consider all relevant duties.

READ TO IMPRESS

Day, R. (2009) Challenging Directors' Bonuses: The Application of Directors' Duties to Service Contracts, CL 374–6

Johnson, S. (2007) Conflicts of Interest and Directors' Duties, 148 (Mar) IHL 38–42

Singla, T. (2007) The Fiduciary Duties of Resigning Directors, 28(9) CL 275–6

www.pearsoned.co.uk/lawexpress

Go online to access more revision support including quizzes to test your knowledge, sample questions with answer guidelines, podcasts you can download, and more!

7 Companies 2:
Shares, resolutions, protection of minority shareholders and charges

Revision checklist

Essential points you should know:

- ☐ The rights and liabilities of shareholders
- ☐ How resolutions of a company are proposed and passed
- ☐ How the law protects minority shareholders
- ☐ The nature of fixed and floating charges
- ☐ The order in which a company's assets are distributed on the winding up of the company

Topic map

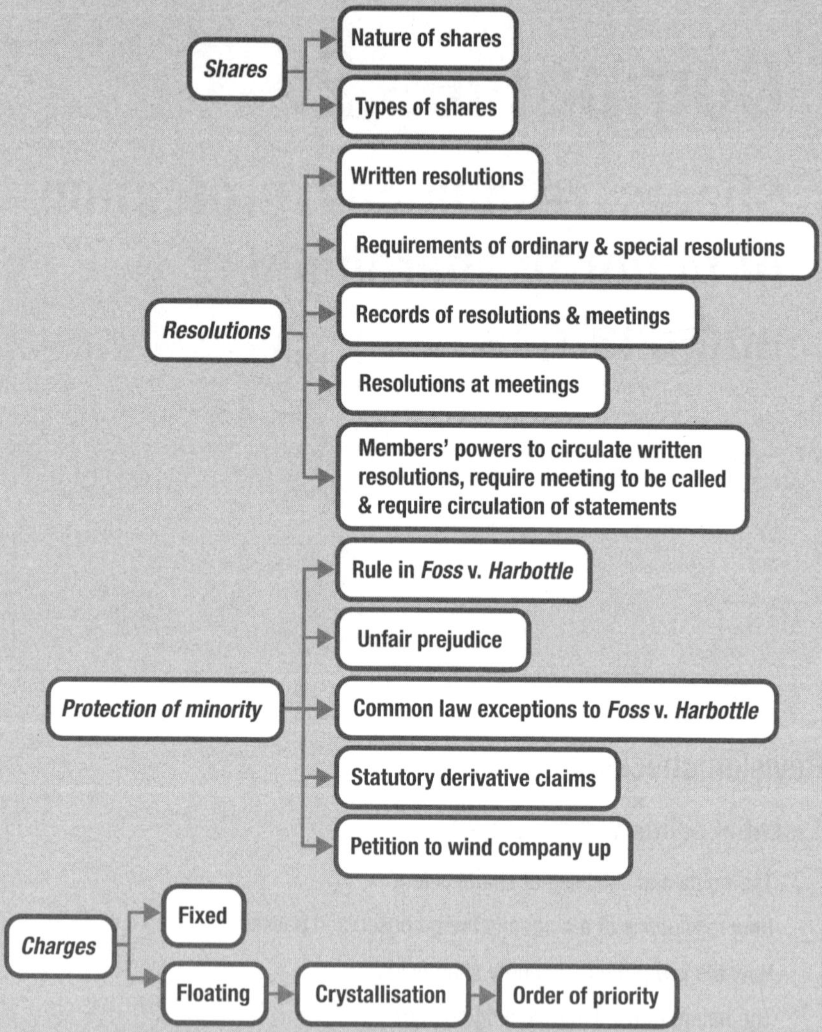

A printable version of this topic map is available from **www.pearsoned.co.uk/lawexpress**

Introduction

A large number of exam questions relate to the rights of minority shareholders.

This chapter considers those rights. The new statutory derivative claim is likely to prove a highly significant development. The chapter also deals with shareholder rights, fixed and floating charges and the order in which a company's assets are distributed when the company is wound up.

ASSESSMENT ADVICE

Essay questions

These tend to ask whether or not minority shareholders are sufficiently protected. You will need to consider the different types of protection which the law gives and also to give your opinion as to whether or not it is adequate.

Problem questions

These often involve a scenario in which one or more minority shareholders are being wronged by the majority. Again, you will need to apply the different methods by which the minority are protected.

Sample question

Could you answer this question? Below is a typical essay question that could arise on this topic. Guidelines on answering the question are included at the end of this chapter, while a sample problem question and guidance on tackling it can be found on the companion website.

ESSAY QUESTION

'Minority shareholders have little control over the way in which a company is run. However, the combined protection afforded to them by statute and the common law should ensure that they are at least treated fairly.'

To what extent do you agree with this view?

Shares

The shareholders (members) of a company do not manage the company – that task is delegated to the directors (see previous chapter). However, they do control the company in that a majority of shareholders can change the directors or wind up the company.

A company's first members consist of those who sign the memorandum of association. Subsequent members acquire shares, either directly from the company or from an existing member.

Generally, payment for shares does not have to be in cash. Shares can be given away or exchanged for goods or services. However, shares in public companies can only be allotted by the company for cash or for an asset which has been independently valued as being worth at least as much as the amount credited as having been paid up.

The nature of shares

Shares confer certain rights and liabilities upon the holder. The liability of a person taking shares in a limited company is to contribute the amount of capital which he or she agreed with the company would be contributed, that is to say to pay the company for the shares if the company issues the shares. Once this amount has been paid, a shareholder has no further liability.

Becoming a shareholder will confer several rights, and the articles may provide for different classes of shares, with different rights attaching to the various classes. The three most important rights are generally the following:

1. to share in a **dividend**, but only if the directors declare a dividend;
2. to vote at company meetings; and
3. to share in the assets of the company if it is wound up.

KEY DEFINITION: Dividend

A dividend is a payment made out of the company's profits to the company members.

You should remember that the articles will spell out the rights attaching to shares and that some shares may not have all of these three rights. The directors declare how much the dividend should be. It is important to remember that dividends can be paid only out of company profits and that even if the company makes a profit, the directors do not need to declare any dividend.

Preference shares

The articles of a company may provide that there will be different classes of shares, with different rights attaching to the various classes. Often a company issues two types of shares: ordinary shares and preference shares. The articles will define the precise rights attaching to preference shares, and obviously these rights will vary from company to company. However, preference shares commonly carry the following rights:

- the dividend payable is expressed as a rate of interest (e.g. 8% per annum);
- any dividend which is not paid in one particular year is payable in full the following year, before ordinary shareholders are paid any dividend;
- the same right to vote as ordinary shares (but often the articles give preference shares no right to vote);
- the right to have the capital which was contributed in return for the shares repaid in full, on the winding up of the company, before the ordinary shares are repaid at all.

Nominal capital and shares issued at a premium

Every share must have a *fixed nominal value*. This represents the minimum amount which the member and the company have agreed should be paid to the company in return for the share, and it is not possible for them to agree that less should in fact be paid.

Money received by the company as **share premium** payments must be put into a share premium account and cannot be paid as a dividend.

KEY DEFINITION: Share premium

A share premium is an extra amount paid to a company for a share, in excess of the nominal value of the share.

Company resolutions and meetings

The members of a company have the power to take certain decisions by passing *resolutions*.

! Don't be tempted to . . .

You should not underestimate the power of the company members. The directors are given the power to manage the company and yet the members have the power to pass resolutions. This tension runs throughout company law. Ultimately, the members have the real power because directors will be bound by resolutions of the members and because members can always pass a resolution dismissing the directors. But while the directors are in office they are the ones who manage the company. Particular problems arise when the directors own the majority of the shares and so have the power to block resolutions proposed by the minority.

In private companies, a resolution of the members may be passed either as a written resolution or at a meeting of the members. The power to pass written resolutions is necessary because private companies are not required to hold meetings of members, although they may choose to do so. A resolution of the members of a public company must be passed at a meeting of the members. Public companies cannot pass written resolutions.

Most resolutions can be passed as *ordinary resolutions*, but some must be passed as special resolutions. A *special resolution* is required by the Companies Act in order to:

- alter the articles of the company;
- alter the company name;
- re-register a company from private to public or from public to private;
- reduce the company's share capital;
- petition for compulsory liquidation of the company.

Written resolutions

Public companies cannot pass written resolutions but private companies can. However, a written resolution may not be used to remove a director, under s. 168, before the expiry of his or her term of office.

REVISION NOTE

The rules on removing a director under s. 168 were considered in the previous chapter (on p. 106).

How is a written resolution passed?

An ordinary resolution is passed as a written resolution when a simple majority of eligible voters (members entitled to vote on the resolution) signify agreement to it. A special resolution is passed as a written resolution when 75% of eligible voters signify agreement to it. Where a special resolution of a private company is passed as a written resolution, the resolution must state that it was proposed as a special resolution. This is so members can see that it is a special resolution, not an ordinary one, which is being proposed. If this is stated, the resolution may only be passed as a special resolution. So if, for example, 60% of eligible members voted in favour of it no resolution would be passed.

Written resolutions can be proposed either by the directors or by eligible members holding at least 5% of the total voting rights entitled to vote on the resolution. When the directors propose a resolution as a written resolution, the company must send a copy of the resolution to every eligible member. This can be done electronically or by sending a hard copy. The copy of the resolution must be accompanied by a statement telling the member how to signify agreement to the resolution and the date by which the resolution must be passed if it is not to lapse.

Members' power to require circulation of written resolutions

KEY STATUTE

Companies Act 2006, s. 292

Section 292(1) allows the members of a private company holding at least 5% of the voting rights, or such lower percentage as the articles specify, to require the company to circulate a written resolution. The members may also require the company to circulate a statement of not more than 1,000 words on the subject matter of the resolution. If a request to circulate a written resolution is properly made, s. 293 requires the company to send the resolution and the accompanying statement to every eligible member, just as if the directors had proposed the resolution.

This is an important right and gives members with at least a 5% shareholding a chance to influence the way in which a company is run.

Resolutions at meetings

The members of both public and private companies can pass either ordinary or special resolutions at a company meeting. Private companies do not need to hold any company meetings but may choose to do so. Public companies must hold at least one meeting, the **AGM**, every financial year and might choose to hold more. Generally, it will be the directors who call company meetings.

An ordinary resolution of the members is passed at a company meeting if a simple majority of eligible members present and voting, in person or by *proxy*, vote in favour of it. A *proxy* is a person who attends the meeting and votes on behalf of a member. Many articles give the chairperson of the meeting the **casting vote** if the votes are split 50 ÷ 50.

KEY DEFINITION: Casting vote

The casting vote is an extra vote given to the chairperson of a meeting (or to someone else) if the votes of all the members who vote are equally split.

A special resolution of the members must be passed by a majority of not less than 75% of members who vote on it.

Members entitled to vote on a resolution proposed at a meeting must be given *written notice* of the meeting and of the proposed resolution. There must be a *quorum* before a meeting can be properly convened. In single member companies the quorum is one qualifying person. As regards all other companies the quorum is two qualifying people. Both members of a company and proxies are regarded as qualifying persons.

When a vote on a *show of hands* is taken at a meeting, each person present, whether a member or a proxy, has one vote. At a vote on a *poll* taken at a company meeting, each share carries one vote. These rules apply unless the articles provide otherwise. Every member has the right to demand a poll and this provision cannot be altered by the articles.

Members' power to require directors to call meetings

KEY STATUTE

Companies Act 2006, s. 303

Section 303 allows 10% of eligible members to require the directors to call a general meeting of the company. In private companies this is reduced to 5%. The members' request must state the general nature of the business to be dealt with at the meeting and may include the text of any resolution to be proposed and voted upon at the meeting.

If the directors are required to hold a meeting under s. 303, s. 304 requires them to call the meeting within 21 days of receiving the request. If they do not do so, then s. 305 allows the members who requested the meeting, or any of them holding at least half of the relevant voting rights, to call a meeting at the company's expense. They must do this within three months of the date on which the directors became subject to the requirement to call a meeting. Any reasonable expenses which the members incurred by requesting a meeting, on account of the directors' failure to duly call the meeting, must be reimbursed by the company. The company will deduct any amount of reimbursement to the members from the directors' fees or remuneration.

Notice of meetings

At least 14 days' notice of a company meeting must be given. However, at least 21 days' notice must be given if the meeting is the AGM of a plc. The company's articles might require longer periods of notice. The members can require a shorter period of notice but this must be agreed by a majority holding the required percentage of shares entitled to attend and vote. As regards a private company the required percentage is 90% or such higher percentage, not exceeding 95%, as the articles may specify. In the case of a public company the requisite percentage is 95%. However, the members can reduce the notice required of an AGM of a public company only by unanimous agreement.

Members' power to require circulation of statements

Section 314 provides that the members of a company may require the company to circulate a statement of not more than 1,000 words with respect to a matter referred to in a proposed resolution to be dealt with at a meeting, or with respect to other business to be dealt with at a meeting. This statement must be circulated to all members entitled to receive notice of a general meeting. The company is required to circulate a statement if either members representing at least 5% of the total voting rights of all members who have a relevant right to vote request it, or if at least 100 members with a relevant right to vote, and holding shares having an average sum paid up of £100 each, request it.

EXAM TIP

If a problem question in an exam describes what percentage of shares the parties have, then the question will probably want you to identify the powers which minority shareholders have. These powers might relate to passing resolutions, having meetings called, having written resolutions circulated or having statements circulated. Demonstrate awareness of the percentage of voting shares which will be needed for each relevant matter and make sure that you apply the law to the problem.

Decisions by sole company member

Whenever the sole member of a single member company takes any decision that takes effect as if taken by the company in general meeting, the member must provide the company with details of that decision. However, this does not apply if the decision was taken by written resolution. Failure to comply is a criminal offence but does not invalidate any decision taken by the sole member.

✓ Make your answer stand out

Why does a single member need to give notice to the company of any decisions taken as if at a general meeting of the company? If a decision of a company is taken at a meeting of the company, will there be a record of that decision? Who could discover what decision was taken?

Records of resolutions and meetings

Section 355 provides that a company must keep records of the following three matters:

1. all resolutions of members passed otherwise than at general meetings;
2. all the minutes of general meetings; and
3. the details provided to the company setting out decisions taken by sole members.

These records must be kept available for inspection at the company's registered office, or at some other place specified in regulations, for at least ten years. Failure to keep them is a criminal offence. Members of the company can inspect the records without having to pay a charge.

Section 30(1) provides that copies of resolutions and agreements affecting a company's constitution must be registered with the Registrar within 15 days of being passed.

REVISION NOTE

In Chapter 6 we saw that s. 17 describes resolutions and agreements affecting a company's constitution as being either special resolutions or agreements or unanimous agreements of the members which would have needed to have been passed as special resolutions.

Protection of minority shareholders

Shareholders who hold fewer than 50% of a company's voting shares can be outvoted on an ordinary resolution. Shareholders who hold 25% of the voting shares, or fewer, cannot block a special resolution. Such minority shareholders can find themselves in a vulnerable position if the majority shareholders elect directors who act in concert against the minority shareholders. Often the majority shareholders elect themselves as directors.

The rule in *Foss* v. *Harbottle*

The position of minority shareholders is not improved by the rule in *Foss* v. *Harbottle* (1843). This rule provides that if a wrong is done to a company, then only the company has the right to sue in respect of that wrong, and that the court will not interfere with the internal management of a company while the company is acting within its powers.

Statutory derivative claims

Section 260 of the 2006 Act allows a member to bring a **derivative claim** on behalf of the company. However, a member bringing a derivative claim must gain permission to continue such a claim from the court.

KEY DEFINITION: Derivative claim

Section 260(1) defines a derivative claim as a claim brought by a member of the company to gain a remedy for the company for some wrong done to the company.

It is important to remember that a derivative claim is brought on behalf of the company rather than on behalf of the aggrieved member. It is also important to remember that if any remedy is ordered it will be a remedy in favour of the company.

A derivative claim may be brought only in respect of two matters:

1. in a cause of action arising from an actual or proposed act or omission which involves negligence, default, breach of duty or breach of trust by a director of the company; or

2. in pursuance of a court order in proceedings under s. 994 for protection for relief from 'unfair prejudice'. (Unfair prejudice is considered below.)

The first category allows a claim to be brought when a director has breached any of the *general statutory duties* set out in ss. 171–177. (See p. 111.)

Section 261(1) provides that a member of a company who brings a derivative claim must apply to the court for permission to continue it. The court has three options:

1. to give permission for the claim to be continued on such terms as it thinks fit;
2. to refuse permission and dismiss the claim; or
3. to adjourn the proceedings and give such directions as it thinks fit.

Section 263(2) deals with whether permission to continue a derivative claim brought in respect of a director's breach of duty should be granted. Permission must be refused in three circumstances:

1. if a person acting in accordance with s. 172 (duty to promote the success of the company) would not seek to continue the claim;
2. where the cause of action arises from an act or omission that is yet to occur, and the act or omission has been authorised by the company;
3. where the cause of action arises from an act or omission that has already occurred but the act or omission was either authorised by the company before it occurred or has been ratified by the company since it occurred.

These are important limitations.

REVISION NOTE

In the previous chapter (on p. 109), we saw the circumstances in which the members could ratify a director's breach of duty and the circumstances in which a conflict of interest could be authorised.

KEY STATUTE

Companies Act 2006, s. 263(3)

Section 263(3) lists six matters which the court should take into account in particular in considering whether to give permission to continue a derivative claim brought in respect of a director's breach of duty. These matters are:

(a) whether the member is acting in good faith in seeking to continue the claim;

(b) the importance that a person acting in accordance with s. 172 (the duty to promote the success of the company) would attach to continuing the claim;

(c) where the cause of action results from an act or omission that is yet to occur, whether the act or omission would be likely to be authorised by the company before it occurs or ratified by the company after it has occurred;

(d) where the cause of action arises from an act or omission that has already occurred, whether the act or omission would be likely to be ratified by the company;

(e) whether the company has decided not to pursue the claim; and

(f) whether the act or omission in respect of which the claim is brought gives rise to a cause of action that the member could pursue in his own right rather than on behalf of the company.

Section 263(4) provides that the court should have particular regard to the views of members of the company who have no personal interest, direct or indirect, in the matter.

Section 264 allows a second member to continue a derivative claim originally brought by another member, if permission from the court is gained.

Statutory protection of members against unfair prejudice

KEY STATUTE

Companies Act 2006, s. 994

Section 994 allows any company member, or the personal representative of a deceased member, to petition the court on the grounds that the affairs of the company are being, or have been, or will be, conducted in a manner which is unfairly prejudicial to the members generally or to particular members, including himself. If the court agrees that the conduct is unfairly prejudicial s. 996(1) allows it to make any order it sees fit to give relief from the unfair prejudice.

Only conduct which is unfair can be within s. 994. Conduct will be unfair if it is contrary to what the parties agreed, either in words or by conduct, taking into account the context and background of the conduct. There will be no unfair prejudice if the majority shareholders offer to buy the shares of the minority at a reasonable price.

Petition for winding up under the Insolvency Act 1986

When a company is wound up it ceases to exist. Any company member can petition the court to wind up a company under ss. 122–124 of the Insolvency Act 1986 on the grounds that it is just and equitable to do so. Whether or not it is just and equitable to wind up a company is a question of fact in every case and will depend upon the circumstances of the case. However, a court would be reluctant to wind up a company if it did not need to.

Common law exceptions to *Foss* v. *Harbottle*

The common law always recognised exceptions to the rule in *Foss* v. *Harbottle*. The courts have been prepared to intervene, despite the rule, in three circumstances:

1. if the personal rights of a member are infringed;
2. if the company proposes to enter into an *ultra vires* transaction; or
3. if there has been a fraud on the minority.

REVISION NOTE

Ultra vires was considered in the previous chapter (on p. 110).

The personal rights of a member have been infringed

A member whose constitutional rights have been infringed will have a contractual right to sue on account of the constitution forming a contract between themselves and the company, and between themselves and the other members. Such an action does not allege any wrong done to the company and so a derivative claim would not be appropriate. For example, if a company refused to allow a member with voting rights to vote at a company meeting, no wrong would have been done to the company but the member's personal rights would have been infringed.

Actions which are *ultra vires*

Earlier we saw that any member of a company has the right to prevent the company from entering into an *ultra vires* transaction, but that if the transaction has already been concluded a member has no power to undo it. However, the members will not have the power to prevent the company entering into an *ultra vires* transaction if the transaction has been approved by special resolution.

Fraud on the minority

Fraud on the minority is not precisely defined, covering a wide range of underhand behaviour. A claim for fraud on the minority will not be possible where the act complained of is merely negligent, rather than fraudulent, and where no personal benefit is conferred on those who control the company and commit the act.

Fraud on the minority was of considerable significance before the introduction of the statutory derivative claim. However, you should remember that a derivative claim can be brought only in respect of a cause of action vested in the company and seeking relief on behalf of the company. Common law fraud on the minority could possibly be important where no wrong is done to the company but the minority members are wronged. However, in such circumstances an action for unfair prejudice would almost always be preferable to an action for fraud on the minority.

Loan capital

A person who lends money to a company will want *security* for the loan. The company can give security by granting a charge over some or all of the company's assets. If the debt is not repaid the lender will be able to sell the charged assets and take what is owed. Companies can give two types of charges: fixed charges and floating charges.

Fixed charges

A fixed charge mortgages certain assets to the creditor. Consequently, the company will not be able to dispose of, or change the nature of, the property charged without the permission of the charge holder.

If a fixed charge is properly created and properly registered its holder will take priority over any subsequent claims to the property charged. A company may grant more than one fixed charge over any particular asset.

Floating charges

A creditor who takes a floating charge takes a company's existing and future assets as security.

KEY CASE

***Re Yorkshire Woolcombers' Association Ltd* [1903] 2 Ch 284 (CA)**

Concerning: the nature of a floating charge

Facts

The facts of this case are lengthy and complicated and to summarise them here would add little to an understanding of the legal principle outlined below.

Legal principle

Romer LJ said that a floating charge had the following three characteristics:

(i) it is a charge on a class of assets of a company, both present and future;

(ii) that class is one which, in the ordinary course of the company's business, would be changing from time to time; and

(iii) it is contemplated that, until some future step is taken by or on behalf of the charge holder, the company may carry on business in the ordinary way as far as concerns the particular class of assets charged.

A floating charge does not attach to any particular items of property until it *crystallises*, so it does not prevent the company from selling the assets over which it is granted.

A third party who acquires property which is subject to a floating charge from the company takes it free of the charge and will own it despite the charge. A third party who acquires property which is subject to a fixed charge will not gain ownership of the property as the company had no power to pass ownership. The fixed charge had already given ownership to the charge holder as security for the loan.

Crystallisation

A company can continue to sell assets over which a floating charge has been granted up until the time of **crystallisation**.

KEY DEFINITION: Crystallisation

Crystallisation is the process by which a floating charge becomes a fixed charge attaching to the assets of the company which are charged at that time. When crystallisation occurs the company is no longer free to dispose of the assets.

Crystallisation occurs automatically:

(a) when a receiver is appointed;

(b) when the company goes into liquidation;

(c) when the company ceases to carry on business;

(d) on the occurrence of an event which the contract creating the charge stipulated would lead to automatic crystallisation.

The contract which created the floating charge commonly provides that any attempt to create a further charge over the property which is the subject of the floating charge will automatically cause the floating charge to crystallise. Crystallisation may also occur when the floating charge holder gives notice that he or she is converting the floating charge into a fixed charge. (This can only be done if the contract which created the charge allows for it.)

Registration of charges

A charge must be registered with the Registrar of Companies, within 21 days after the date of its creation. If a charge is not registered it will be invalid, although the charge holder will still be able to sue on the debt as an unsecured creditor.

The company must also keep a copy of the documents which created the charge, as well as a register of all the charges affecting its property. This register gives brief details of each charge (the property charged, the amount of the charge and the person entitled to it). Members and creditors can inspect this register free of charge; others may be charged a small fee. If a charge is not entered on the company's register of charges the directors and secretary may be fined, but the charge will not be rendered invalid.

Priority of charges

As regards properly registered charges, the order of priority is as follows:

1. A fixed charge has immediate effect from the moment it was created. It ranks higher than existing floating charges unless the floating charge expressly prohibits the creation of another charge over the same property and the person taking the later fixed charge knew that this was the case. (Registration is not enough on its own to amount to actual notice of the prohibition.)
2. Floating charges only attach to property from the moment of crystallisation.
3. Floating charges generally rank amongst themselves in order of priority of creation. This is not the case where the debenture securing the first floating charge provides that a later floating charge may have priority.

Distribution of a company's assets when the company is wound up

After the holders of fixed charges have called them in, the Insolvency Act sets out the order in which the company's assets must be distributed. Each class of creditors is paid in full before the class below is paid anything. If there are insufficient funds to pay a class in full, all members of that class receive the same percentage of what they are owed.

The order of payment is as follows:

- the liquidator's remuneration and the costs and expenses of winding up;
- the preferential creditors at the time of winding up;
- floating charges created before 15 September 2003;
- top-sliced assets for distribution to the unsecured creditors (see p. 133);
- floating charges created on or after 15 September 2003;
- the unsecured creditors;
- sums due to members but not yet paid, for example dividends declared but not yet paid;
- the members of the company, as set out in the articles of association.

Preferential creditors

Preferential creditors are owed money in relation to the following types of debts:

- contributions to occupational pension schemes;
- unpaid wages of up to £800 per employee;
- unpaid holiday pay;
- loans used to pay wages or holiday pay.

Top slicing

Top slicing applies to floating charges created on or after 15 September 2003. This means that the liquidator must set aside a certain percentage of the assets which would otherwise be payable to floating charge holders so that this amount can be paid to the unsecured creditors. The amount which must be set aside for the unsecured creditors is 50% of the first £10,000 (after payment of the costs of realising the company's assets and the preferential creditors), then 20% of the remainder, the fund having a ceiling of £600,000. However, if the value of the company's net property (after the payment of those ranking in priority to floating charges) is less than £10,000 the liquidator does not have to distribute the funds to the unsecured creditors if this would be disproportionate to the costs of doing so.

Putting it all together

Answer guidelines

See the essay question at the start of the chapter.

Approaching the question

- You should explain that a company is run by its board of directors and that minority shareholders will generally not have the power to appoint or remove directors.
- You should explain that minority shareholders cannot prevent ordinary resolutions from being passed and can prevent special resolutions from being passed only if they hold more than 25% of the voting shares.
- You should explain the protection which statute and the common law give to minority shareholders.
- You should comment on whether this protection ensures that minority shareholders are treated fairly.

Important points to include

You should include the following matters:

- the vulnerable position of minority shareholders, in the light of the rule in *Foss* v. *Harbottle*;
- the powers of members to circulate a written resolution under s. 292 and to require the directors to call a meeting under s. 303;

- the new statutory derivative claim;
- unfair prejudice under s. 994;
- the common law exceptions to *Foss* v. *Harbottle*;
- an evaluation of the extent to which you agree with the quotation.

✓ Make your answer stand out

Make examples of how the minority could be unfairly treated. Deal with derivative claims in detail, but explain that they can only gain a remedy for a wrong done to the company. Explain the circumstances in which a claim for unfair prejudice is likely to be the best hope for a wronged minority shareholder. This will impress the examiner because, as we have seen, sometimes one of these courses of action is more appropriate than the other. Don't forget to give your evaluation as to the extent to which the quotation is correct. That, after all, is what the question asked you to do.

READ TO IMPRESS

Almadani M. (2009) Derivative Actions: Does the Companies Act Offer a Way Forward? CL 131–40

Hirt, H. (2004) Ratification of Breaches of Directors' Duties: The Implications of the Reform Proposed Regarding the Availability of Derivative Actions, 25(7) CL 197–212

Lightman, D. (2007) The Companies Act 2006: A Nutshell Guide to Changes to the Derivative Claim, 26(1) CJQ 37–9

Omar P. (2009) In the Wake of the Companies Act 2006: An Assessment of the Potential Impact of the Reforms to Company Law, ICCLR 44–55

www.pearsoned.co.uk/lawexpress

Go online to access more revision support including quizzes to test your knowledge, sample questions with answer guidelines, podcasts you can download, and more!

8 Partnership, limited liability partnership and sole trading

Revision checklist

Essential points you should know:

- [ ] The main differences between trading as a partnership, a limited liability partnership (LLP) and a sole trader
- [ ] The nature of a partnership and of a limited liability partnership
- [ ] The extent to which partners, and members of LLPs, are agents of each other and are liable for each other's torts
- [ ] The statutory rules relating to partners' and LLP members' relationship with each other
- [ ] How assets are applied when a partnership or LLP is wound up

Topic Map

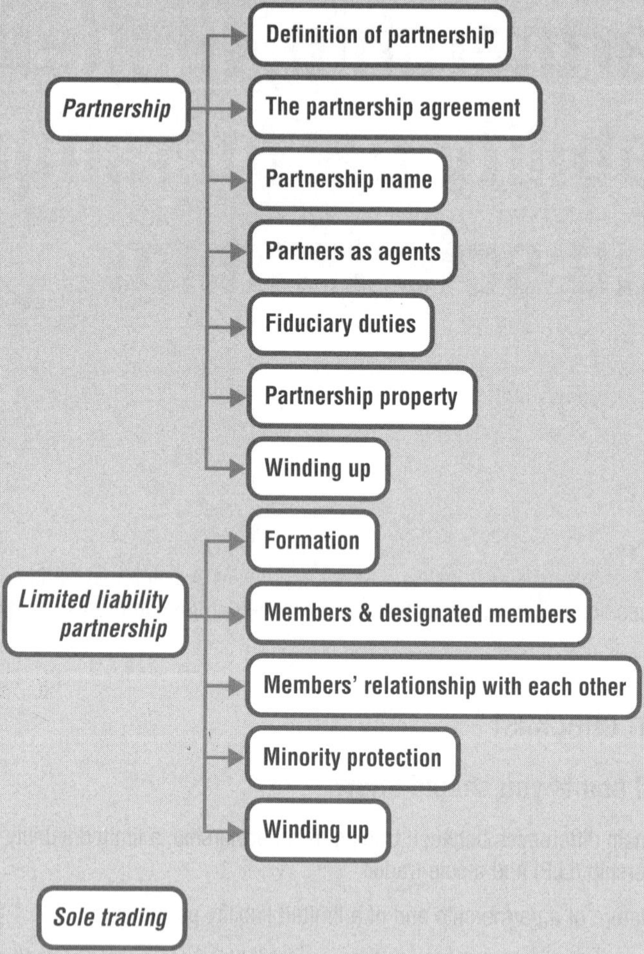

A printable version of this topic map is available from **www.pearsoned.co.uk/lawexpress**

Introduction

Many exam questions require an application of the law relating to partnerships or limited liability partnerships.

A business which does not trade as a company must trade as a partnership, a limited liability partnership or a sole trader. This chapter considers each of these different ways of trading.

ASSESSMENT ADVICE

Questions might just be about partnership or just be about limited liability partnership. Alternatively, they might be about both forms of trading, or they might ask you to compare trading as a partner, as an LLP or as a limited company.

Questions frequently deal with:

- the ways in which other partners, or an LLP, can be made liable by one individual partner or individual member of an LLP;
- the relationship between partners, or between members of an LLP; or
- distribution of assets on a winding up.

Sample question

Could you answer this question? Below is a typical problem question that could arise on this topic. Guidelines on answering the question are included at the end of this chapter, while a sample essay question and guidance on tackling it can be found on the companion website.

PROBLEM QUESTION

Xavier, Yasmin and Zak are in partnership together as antique dealers. They have no formal partnership agreement. However, they have agreed that Zak should never buy anything other than pottery on behalf of the firm. In contradiction of this, Zak bought a painting for the firm for £35,000 at a local auction. He thought that it was by Picasso but it is in fact a fake worth about £100. Last week a customer was injured in the shop when Yasmin negligently dropped a bronze statue on his toe. Xavier and Yasmin each contributed capital of £10,000 when the firm was created. Zak contributed no capital. This capital of £20,000 has been lost and, taking all liabilities into account, the firm has further debts of £10,000. This figure does not include the £35,000 which Zak agreed to pay for the painting, or the £15,000 damages which will need to be paid to the injured customer.

Advise the three partners of their legal positions.

Partnership

Definition

This definition makes it plain that a **partnership** is not a separate legal person, in the way that a company is. A partnership (also called a firm) is merely a relationship between the partners, who carry on a business together. The business must be carried on for the benefit of all of the partners and they must intend to make a profit.

KEY DEFINITION: Partnership

Section 1(1) of the Partnership Act 1890 defines partnership as the relation which subsists between persons carrying on a business in common with a view of profit.

Partners as agents

KEY STATUTE

Partnership Act 1890, s. 5

Section 5 of the PA 1890 is a long section which begins by providing that every partner is an agent of the firm and his other partners for the purpose of the business of the partnership. This means that every partner can make contracts on behalf of the firm and that these contracts will be binding on the firm and on all of the other partners. However, this power to make contracts is not absolute. Section 5 allows a partner to bind the firm and fellow partners only if the following conditions are satisfied:

- the contract must appear to have been made on behalf of the firm;
- the contract must have been the type of contract which the firm would usually make; and
- the contract must also have been made in the usual way one would expect such a contract to be made.

Figure 8.1

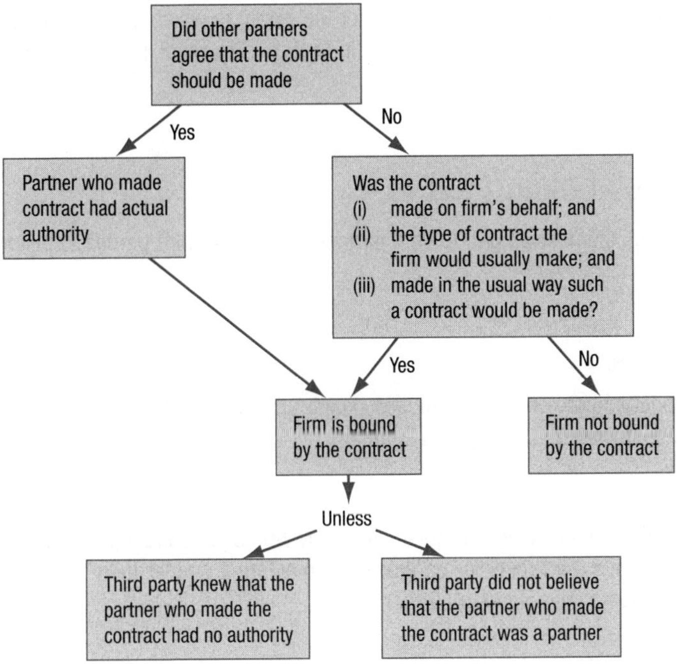

Liability in tort

The liability of the firm, and of fellow partners, for the torts of another partner is governed by s. 10 of the PA 1890, the effect of which is shown in Figure 8.2.

Figure 8.2

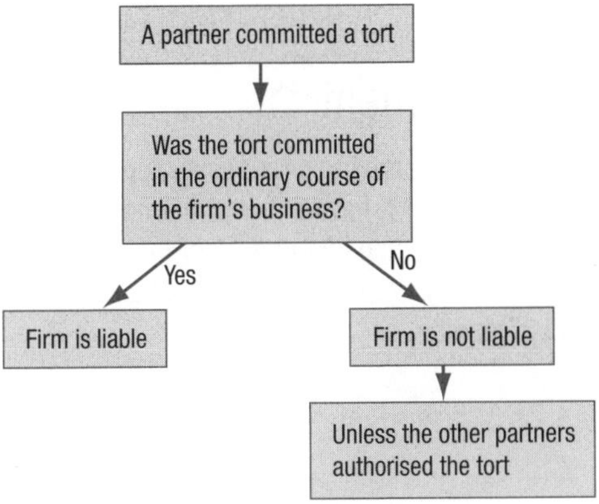

EXAM TIP

Many exam questions want you to consider the extent to which one partner can make other partners liable, either in contract or in tort. Use Figures 8.1 and 8.2 to structure your answer.

Liability by holding out

A person 'holds themselves out' to be a partner if they lead third parties to believe that they are a partner.

REVISION NOTE

For the requirements of holding out, see Chapter 6 (on p. 108), in relation to holding out a person as managing director of a company.

A person can hold themselves out as a partner by words or conduct. Also, if a person *knowingly* allows a third party to represent that they are a partner then they will be regarded as having held out as a partner.

KEY STATUTE

Partnership Act 1890, s. 14

A person who is not a partner in a firm will not be liable for the firm's debts. But if a person holds himself out as being a partner, or knowingly allows himself to be held out as being a partner, and this causes a third party to give credit to the firm, s. 14 of the PA 1890 provides that the person who held himself out to be a partner will be liable as if he really was a partner.

The partnership agreement

People become partners merely by carrying on a business together with the intention of making a profit. Most partnerships will have a formal partnership agreement, generally known as a deed of partnership. Sections 24 and 25 of the PA 1890 make implied rules (set out in Figure 8.3), which will govern the partners' relationship with each other unless the partners have agreed otherwise.

Figure 8.3

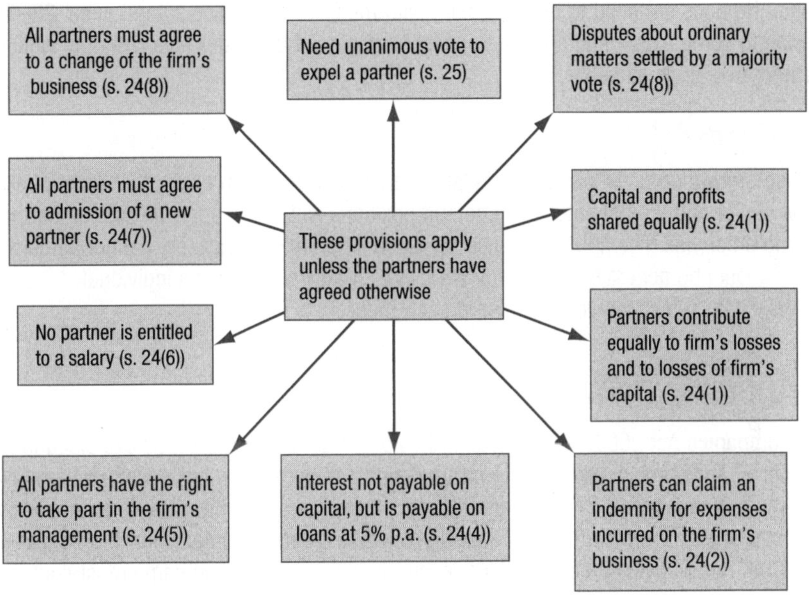

Fiduciary duties

KEY STATUTE

Partnership Act 1890, ss. 28–30

28 Partners are bound to render true accounts and full information of all things affecting the partnership to any partner or his legal representatives.

29 Every partner must account to the firm for any benefit derived by him without the consent of the other partners from any transaction concerning the partnership, or from any use by him of the partnership property, name or business connection.

30 If a partner, without the consent of the other partners, carries on any business of the same nature as and competing with that of the firm, he must account for and pay over to the firm all profits made by him in that business.

The duties set out in ss. 28–30 of the PA 1890 are *fiduciary duties*. The partners cannot agree to do away with them altogether. However, it is permissible for partners to compete with the firm, or use the firm's assets to make a profit, as long as all the other partners consent to this. Section 29 is similar to s. 30. The difference is that under s. 30 the partner is liable just because he competes with the firm. He does not need to use partnership property or assets. Under s. 29 a partner is liable for misusing partnership property or assets. He does not need to be competing with the firm. The duties set out in ss. 28–30 overlap to some extent and are just specific examples of the wider fiduciary duty which partners owe each other.

EXAM TIP

When answering questions on the relationship of partners with each other remember that ss. 24 and 25 just set out the default positions which will apply unless the partners agree otherwise. The fiduciary duties are quite different. The partners cannot agree that they should be generally done away with, even if they can sanction individual transactions which would otherwise breach them.

Partnership name

The Companies Act 2006 makes certain rules about company names, as explained in Chapter 6. These rules also apply to partnerships if they carry on business in a name other than the surnames of all the partners. If the partners merely add their first names, or their initials, to their surnames they will not be subject to the rules contained in the Companies Act 2006. But if anything else is added, even the words '& Co.', the name must comply with the Act.

Section 1193 of the CA 2006 makes it a criminal offence to use names which would suggest a connection with government or local authorities. The Secretary of State can grant permission for such names to be used.

Section 1202 of the CA 2006 states that a notice containing the names of all the partners must be prominently displayed at any business premises to which the customers or suppliers have access. An address at which documents can be served on each named partner must also be displayed. If s. 1202 is not complied with, then in some circumstances contracts made by the firm may be unenforceable by the partners.

A *passing-off* action can be brought to prevent partners from trading under a name which is too similar to that of another business. Such an action will succeed only if the use of the name is likely to take trade away from the other business or cause confusion between the two businesses.

Partnership property

Partnership property belongs to all of the partners, who hold it on trust for each other. No individual partner owns partnership property. When a firm is wound up the partnership property will be used to pay the debts and liabilities of the firm. Property is partnership property if:

- it was brought into the firm as partnership property; or
- it was bought with the firm's money as partnership property; or
- it was acquired for the purposes of the firm and in the usual course of the firm's business.

The *goodwill* of the firm is partnership property and might be one of the firm's most valuable assets.

! Don't be tempted to . . .

You should not think that it is easy to define goodwill. Accountants might define it as the amount by which the market value of a business exceeds the value of its individual assets. Various legal definitions have been put forward.

In *Trego* v. *Hunt* (1896) Lord MacNaughten defined goodwill as 'the whole advantage, whatever it may be, of the reputation and connection of the firm'.

In *Hill* v. *Fearis* (1905) Warrington J said that it was 'the advantage, whatever it may be, which a person gets by continuing to carry on, and being entitled to represent to the outside world that he is carrying on, a business which has been carried on for some time previously'.

The goodwill is an asset of the business, which is valued and sold when the business is sold. Once the goodwill has been sold, for the benefit of all of the partners, those partners will not be able to use the firm's name or solicit its customers.

Winding up

A firm will cease to exist when it is wound up. A winding up can be brought about either by the partners themselves or by the court.

When a firm is wound up its assets will be gathered in and distributed. A firm is solvent if it can pay all of its debts. Just because a firm has made a loss, and therefore lost some of the capital contributed by the partners, this does not necessarily mean that the firm is insolvent. If the firm is solvent when it is liquidated, s. 44 of the PA 1890 provides that payments are made in the following order:

1. All outsiders will be fully paid what they are owed.
2. Loans made by partners will be repaid.

3. The partners will be repaid the capital which they contributed to the firm. If there is not enough capital to repay all of the partners, the partners must contribute to the lost capital in the same proportion as they were to share profits (unless they had agreed otherwise).
4. Any surplus will be paid to the partners in the ratio in which they were to share profits.

The firm will be insolvent if it does not have enough assets to pay its debts. Section 44 of the PA 1890 provides that losses must be paid in the following order:

1. out of profits;
2. out of capital; and
3. if necessary, by the partners individually in the proportion in which they were to share profits.

If some partners are personally insolvent, and so cannot pay their share, the other partners will take over liability to pay the insolvent partner's share. Partners may be made bankrupt if they cannot pay their share.

Limited liability partnership

Two or more persons can trade together as a limited liability partnership (LLP). An LLP is quite different from an ordinary partnership because, like a company, it is a separate legal entity in its own right.

People who participate in an LLP are known as members of the LLP and not as partners. LLPs have some of the features of an ordinary partnership but are closer to limited companies. The main similarity with a limited company is that an LLP is a corporate body and so, in general, only the LLP itself will be liable for the debts of the LLP. However, LLPs do not pay corporation tax, as companies do. Instead the members are taxed individually on their share of the profits.

✓ Make your answer stand out

One of the main reasons why LLPs were introduced was to protect firms of accountants and solicitors, which previously had to trade as ordinary partnerships. Partners in ordinary firms have unlimited liability for the firm's debts. Members of LLPs do not. Should it be possible for the members of such LLPs to have limited liability? If so, why should they not just trade as companies?

Formation of LLPs

LLPs, like companies, are incorporated by registration with the Registrar of Companies. There must be at least two members of an LLP, one of whom at least must be a designated member (see below). It is not possible to have a single person LLP. The rules relating to prohibited names, the places in which a name must be displayed and the way in which the LLP name can be changed are identical to the rules which apply to limited companies.

Members and designated members

LLPs do not have partners, directors or shareholders. Instead they have members and designated members. Being a member of an LLP is similar to being a partner in an ordinary partnership. However, every LLP must always have at least one designated member, whose duties are similar to those imposed on the officers (the directors and the secretary) of a limited company.

Members as agents

KEY STATUTE

Limited Liability Partnerships Act 2000, ss. 6 and 4(4)

Section 6 of the LLPA 2000 is very similar to s. 5 of the Partnership Act 1890. There are only two significant differences. First, it is the LLP which will be bound by the contract, not each of the members. Second, there is no requirement that the contract should have been the type of contract which the LLP would usually make. The effect of s. 5 of the PA 1890 was set out earlier in this chapter in Figure 8.1.

Section 4(4) of the LLPA 2000 is similar to s. 10 of the Partnership Act 1890, which is set out earlier in this chapter in Figure 8.2. It makes an LLP liable for the torts of its members if these were committed during the course of the business of the LLP or with the authority of the LLP.

Members' relationship with each other

Regulation 7 of the Limited Liability Partnership Regulations 2001 sets out default provisions, which govern the members' relationship with each other. These will apply unless the members make their own provisions instead.

There are ten default provisions in reg. 7. The first seven are virtually identical to the first seven provisions made by s. 24 of the Partnership Act 1890, which were considered earlier in this chapter. However, it should be noted that the members of an LLP do not have to share in the losses of the LLP because the LLP is a corporate body with a legal identity of its own. The final three default provisions are very similar to ss. 28–30 of the Partnership Act 1890. Regulation 8 is virtually identical to s. 25 of the Partnership Act. Sections 24, 25, 28, 29 and 30 of the Partnership Act 1890 were considered earlier in this chapter (on pp. 140–2).

Minority protection

Any member of an LLP can petition the court to wind up the LLP under s. 122 of the Insolvency Act 1986. Any member also has the right to petition the court claiming unfair prejudice under s. 994 of the Companies Act 2006. Both of these provisions were considered in Chapter 7, in relation to limited companies (see p. 128).

The Company Directors Disqualification Act 1986, considered in Chapter 6 (at p. 107), applies to both members and designated members.

Winding up of limited liability partnerships

REVISION NOTE

LLPs are wound up in the same way as companies. After a winding up the assets of the LLP are applied in the same order as would be the assets of a company (see p. 132).

In addition, members of an LLP can agree with the other members or with the LLP that they will be personally liable for the LLP's debts up to a certain amount.

Members of an LLP can leave the business by giving notice. However, as this does not automatically dissolve the LLP, the member who leaves will have no automatic right to share in the assets of the LLP.

Sole trading

A sole trader is in business on his or her own. Sole traders often employ others but the business is not run for the benefit of these others. If a sole trader and another carry on a business together to try to make a profit, which they intend to share, then a partnership will have been created. Sole traders are personally liable for any debts of the business. A person who wishes to run a business for his or her own benefit does not have to operate as a sole trader. Instead he or she can register the business as a limited company, with no other shareholders or directors, rather than trading as a sole trader.

Putting it all together

Answer guidelines

See the problem question at the start of the chapter.

Approaching the question

You will need to deal with the following matters:

- Are all of the partners liable for the £35,000 which Zak agreed to pay for the painting?
- Are all of the partners liable for the injury to the customer which Yasmin caused?
- To what extent will each partner be liable for the losses of the firm?
- How much will each partner lose?

Important points to include

- You will need to apply s. 5 PA 1890 to the contract for the painting. Use Figure 8.1 to help you do this.
- You will need to apply s. 10 PA 1890 to see whether all of the partners are liable for Yasmin's negligence. Use Figure 8.2 to help you do this.
- Apply s. 44 PA 1890 to see how each partner stands as regards the losses of capital and the firm's debts.

✓ Make your answer stand out

Deal with each issue in turn. Show that you understand the relevant sections of the PA 1890 and apply these clearly to the problem. This will gain good marks, whereas a mere repetition of the sections will not.

READ TO IMPRESS

Gretton, G. (1987) Who Owns Partnership Property? 2(6) JR 163–78

Henning, J. (2005) The Deadlocked Limited Liability Partnership – Arbitration or Winding Up? 26(11) CL 289–90

Vollans, T. (2004) Section 5, Partnership Act Clarified, 25(5/6) BLR 117–19

www.pearsoned.co.uk/lawexpress

Go online to access more revision support including quizzes to test your knowledge, sample questions with answer guidelines, podcasts you can download, and more!

9

Employment 1:

The contract of employment, employment rights, dismissal and redundancy

Revision checklist

Essential points you should know:

- [ ] How to distinguish employees and independent contractors
- [ ] The statutory rights of employees
- [ ] The difference between unfair dismissal and wrongful dismissal
- [ ] The remedies available for unfair dismissal and for wrongful dismissal
- [ ] The circumstances in which an employee will have been made redundant, and the statutory remedies available for redundancy

Topic map

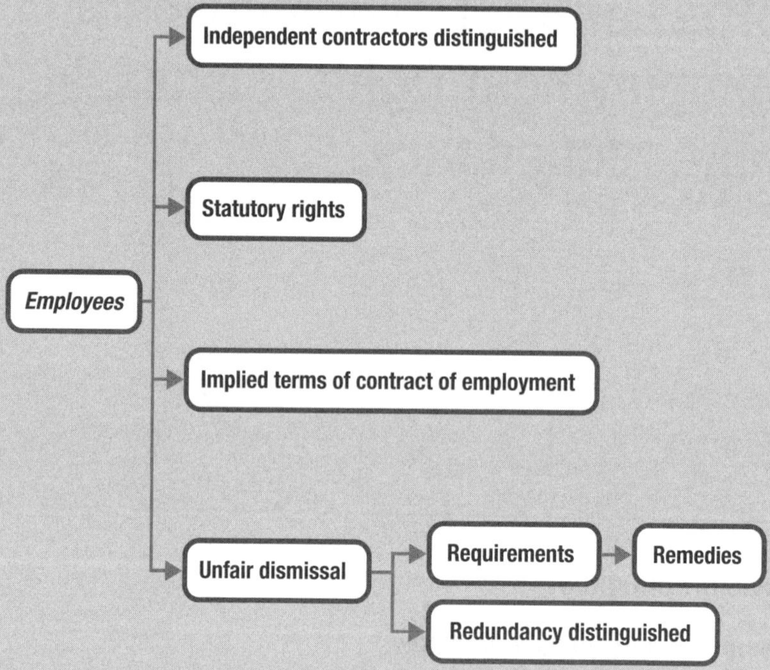

A printable version of this topic map is available from **www.pearsoned.co.uk/lawexpress**

Introduction

Many exam questions concern the statutory rights of employees, particularly when they have been dismissed or made redundant. This chapter focuses on these rights. People work for others either as employees or as independent contractors. If they work as employees they will have a contract of employment. Certain terms are always implied into such contracts. Employees also gain various statutory rights.

A dismissed **employee** might be able to make a claim for unfair or **wrongful dismissal**, or possibly for both. However, unfair dismissal is not the same as wrongful dismissal and the two matters must be considered separately. An employee who is made redundant will be entitled to a statutory redundancy payment. But redundancy can arise only if an employee is dismissed for one of six specific reasons. Most dismissed employees are not made redundant.

ASSESSMENT ADVICE

Essay questions

Make sure that you answer the question. Does it require you to distinguish between employees and independent contractors, or not? Is it about one right of an employee or about several? If the question asks for your opinion, make sure that you use cases and statutes to justify your opinion.

Problem questions

Read the question. As the statutory rights are available only to employees, a question might require you to say whether a person is an employee or not. But if it is obvious that he or she is, don't waste time on this. Deal only with relevant statutory rights. If a question is on unfair dismissal or redundancy, and states for how long a person has been an employee, show that you understand the way in which a basic award or statutory redundancy payment will be calculated. If the statutory dismissal or grievance procedures are relevant, make sure that you explain them.

Sample question

Could you answer this question? Below is a typical essay question that could arise on this topic. Guidelines on answering the question are included at the end of this chapter, while a sample problem question and guidance on tackling it can be found on the companion website.

ESSAY QUESTION

'Unfair dismissal is not the same thing as redundancy. An employer cannot call a dismissed employee redundant if that employee has in fact been unfairly dismissed. However, it must be borne in mind that not all dismissals are unfair.'

Explain whether you consider this quotation to be true. Explain also why an employer might want to say that an employee who has in fact been unfairly dismissed has been made redundant.

Employees and independent contractors distinguished

There are three main reasons to distinguish **employees** from **independent contractors**:

1. Terms which are implied into contracts of employment are not implied into the contracts of independent contractors.
2. Employers can be vicariously liable (see p. 93) for the torts of their employees if they are committed during the course of their employment.
3. Several statutes give protection to employees but not to independent contractors.

KEY DEFINITION: Employee and independent contractor

An employee is a person employed under a contract of employment, also known as a contract of service.

An independent contractor is a person who makes a contract to provide a service, but does not do so as an employee.

! Don't be tempted to . . .

You should not think that it is always easy to distinguish between employees and independent contractors. The courts have used various tests to tell the difference.

However, you should remember that the question is one of fact and so no single test can be used to find the answer. A summary of the leading cases would indicate that the following matters indicate a contract of employment:

- The person for whom the work is done dictates not only what work must be done but also the way in which it must be done.
- The worker is employed as part of the business and his or her work is done as an integral part of the business.
- The terms of the contract are generally consistent with a contract of employment (considering matters such as who pays the worker's tax and what type of National Insurance contributions are paid).
- The worker provides his or her own work and skill in return for a wage or other payment.
- The worker does not provide equipment, hire helpers or take a financial risk.
- The worker does not stand to make a large profit from sound management of the performance of the work.
- A worker can be an employee even if he or she agrees to be called an independent contractor.

Terms implied into a contract of employment

Terms are implied into a contract of employment as a matter of law. Some implied terms impose obligations on the employee and some impose obligations on the employer.

Implied obligations of the employee

These are as follows:

- to show mutual respect to the employer;
- to faithfully serve the employer;
- to obey lawful and reasonable orders;
- to use reasonable care and skill;
- not to accept bribes;
- not to reveal confidential information.

Implied obligations of the employer

These are as follows:

- to show mutual respect to the employee;
- to provide work, or pay the employee if there is no work;
- to pay wages;
- not to reveal confidential information;
- to indemnify employees for expenses and costs reasonably incurred;
- to insure the employee;
- to take reasonable care and skill in preparing a reference. (However, an employer has no duty to provide a reference.)

Statutory provisions conferring rights on employees

Written statement of employment particulars

Section 1 of the Employment Rights Act 1996 (ERA 1996) requires an employer to provide all employees with a written statement of employment particulars.

Itemised pay statements

Section 8(1) of the ERA 1996 requires employers to provide a written itemised pay statement when wages or salary are paid.

Maternity rights

Unless the contract terms give a more generous entitlement, the Maternity and Parental Leave Regulations 1999 give all female employees a statutory right to 52 weeks' maternity leave. An employee is entitled to statutory maternity pay for up to 39 weeks, beginning when she goes on ordinary maternity leave.

Paternity leave and pay

Section 80A of the Employment Act 2002 gives fathers of newly born children the right to paternity leave and paternity pay which can either be for one week or for two consecutive weeks. To qualify the father must have at least 26 weeks' continuous employment.

Adoption leave and pay

When a couple adopt a child, s. 75A of the Employment Act 2002 entitles one member of the couple to take 52 weeks' adoption leave with statutory adoption pay for up to 39 weeks. To qualify the person taking the leave must have at least 26 weeks' continuous employment.

Parental leave and time off for dependants

The Maternity and Parental Leave Regulations 1999 give an employee with at least one year's continuous employment the right to take up to 18 weeks' unpaid parental leave, in respect of each child, to look after his or her child or to make arrangements for the child's welfare. The leave must be taken before the child's fifth birthday (or 18th birthday if the child is disabled). All employees are entitled under s. 57A of the ERA 1996 to take time off work to look after dependants in an emergency.

Flexible working for parents

Section 80F of the Employment Act 2002 gives parents and carers the right to apply for flexible working. Employers will have a statutory duty to consider these applications seriously but there is no automatic right to work flexibly. Only employees with at least 26 weeks' continuous employment can apply.

Transfer of employees

The Transfer of Undertakings (Protection of Employment) Regulations 2006 (TUPE) provide that when a business is transferred from one employer to another as a going concern the contracts of employment of all the employees are also transferred. These contracts then take effect as if made between the individual employees and the new employer.

National minimum wage

The National Minimum Wage Act 1998 introduced new rights to a national minimum wage. The amount of the minimum wage depends upon the employee's age and is increased in line with inflation.

Working Time Regulations 1998

These regulations provide that a worker's working time should not be more than 48 hours, including overtime, in each seven-day period when calculated over any 17-week period. It is the employer's duty to see that the limit is not exceeded. Any days which are taken off as annual holiday, sick leave or maternity leave are regarded as excluded days. An employee can choose to opt out of the regulations.

Unfair dismissal

The following conditions must be satisfied if a claim for unfair dismissal is to be successfully made:

- an employee must have been dismissed;
- the dismissed employee must have had at least two years' continuous employment;
- the claim must have been brought within three months of the date of termination;
- the dismissal must have been unfair.

There must have been a dismissal

There can be a claim for unfair **dismissal** only if an employee is dismissed.

KEY DEFINITION: Dismissal

Section 95 of the ERA 1996 provides that an employee is dismissed if:

- the employer terminates the contract, with or without notice;
- a fixed-term contract ends and is not renewed; or
- the employee terminates the contract on the grounds of the employer's unreasonable conduct. (This last method is known as constructive dismissal.)

Continuous employment

Only employees with at least two years' continuous employment can claim unfair dismissal. Independent contractors cannot claim. Section 212(1) of the ERA 1996 defines the weeks which count towards continuous employment as any week during the whole or part of which an employee's relations with his or her employer are governed by a contract of employment.

Section 212(3) of the ERA 1996 allows up to 26 weeks to count towards continuous employment even if the employee was absent due to illness, or a temporary cessation of work, or absent by arrangement or custom. Weeks lost through industrial action do not break the continuity of employment, although they do not count as weeks of continuous employment either. If a business is taken over by a new employer as a going concern, weeks worked for the old employer count as weeks worked for the new employer.

Claim brought within three months

An employee's employment is regarded as having ended on the effective date of termination. Generally, this is the date on which the employee actually stopped working for the employer. A claim must be brought within three months of this date.

Dismissal must have been unfair

A dismissal will be unfair unless the employer can prove that it was made on one of the following grounds:

- the capability or qualifications of the employee to do the kind of work he or she was employed to do;
- the conduct of the employee;
- the redundancy of the employee;
- the employee could not continue to work in his or her job without contravening a statutory duty or restriction;
- some other substantial reason.

If the employer can prove that the dismissal was made on one of the above grounds, the employment tribunal must then decide whether it actually was fair or unfair. Section 98(4) of the ERA 1996 provides that this will depend upon whether, in the circumstances, the employer acted reasonably or unreasonably in treating the reason for the dismissal as a sufficient reason for dismissing the employee.

KEY CASE

***Post Office* v. *Foley* [2000] IRLR 827 (CA)**

Concerning: the approach to be taken when deciding whether the employer acted reasonably

Facts

The facts of this case are lengthy and complicated and to summarise them here would add little to an understanding of the legal principle outlined below. Remember that examiners are usually looking for an understanding of the ratio and legal principle and that reciting the facts in an exam will not improve your grade.

Legal principle

The Court of Appeal confirmed the *band of reasonable responses* test. Under this test, the employer will have acted reasonably if he or she took a view which a reasonable employer might have taken, even if a different reasonable employer might have taken a different view.

This band of reasonable responses test seems very favourable to the employer.

Automatically unfair dismissals

If a dismissal is automatically unfair, the tribunal does not need to consider whether it was fair or unfair. A dismissal is automatically unfair if it was:

- on the grounds of the employee trying to enforce a relevant statutory right;
- on the grounds of pregnancy;
- for being a member of a trade union;
- for being on strike, if the dismissal occurred in the first eight weeks of the strike;
- for being a union representative;
- for carrying out health and safety duties;
- for refusing to work on Sundays (some workers do not have this protection);
- in connection with a transfer of undertakings from one employer to another.

EXAM TIP

Figure 9.1 shows the ACAS disciplinary procedure, which must be complied with before a dismissal is made. Figure 9.2 shows the ACAS grievance procedure, which an employee must initiate before claiming constructive dismissal in front of a tribunal.

If either procedure is not complied with, an employment tribunal can increase or reduce the compensation payable by up to 25%. Whether it is increased or reduced will depend upon whether the failure to comply was the fault of the employer or the employee.

Figure 9.1

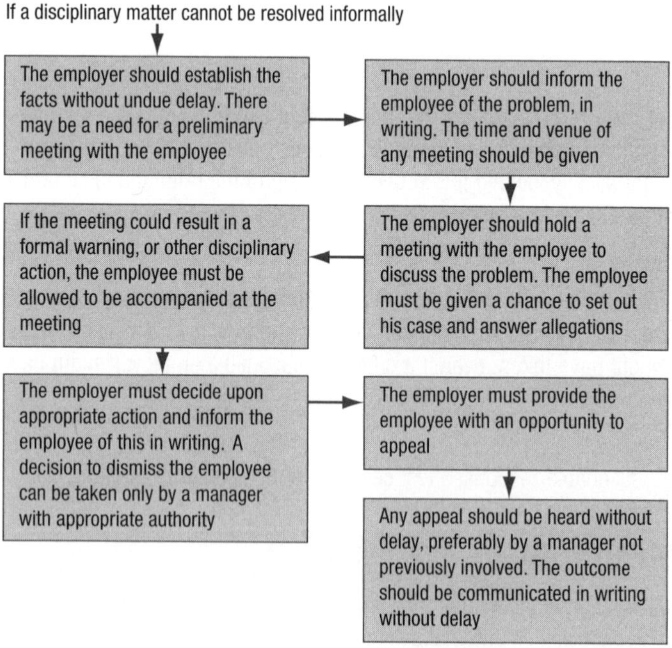

Figure 9.2

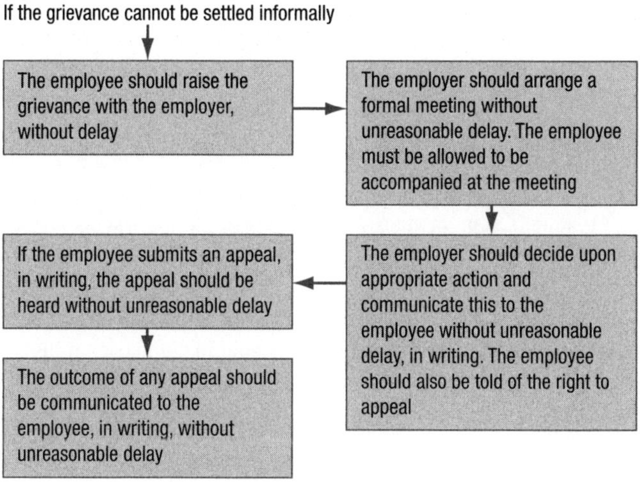

Remedies for unfair dismissal

There are three remedies for unfair dismissal: reinstatement, re-engagement and compensation.

1. *Reinstatement* means that the employee is treated as if there had been no dismissal. It is rarely ordered.
2. *Re-engagement* means that the employee is given a different job which is similar to the old job.
3. *Compensation* consists of a **basic award**, with the possibility of a compensatory award or an additional award.

KEY DEFINITION: Basic award

An award of money, calculated by reference to the employee's weekly wage and length of employment, to which all unfairly dismissed employees are entitled.

The *basic award* is calculated as follows.

First, the relevant number of complete years' continuous employment is calculated. Then this figure is multiplied by a multiplier and the normal week's pay.

1. For years worked while under the age of 22, each year of continuous employment entitles the employee to 0.5 of a week's pay.
2. For years worked while over 22 and under 41 years old, each year of continuous employment entitles the employee to 1 week's pay.
3. For years worked while the employee was over the age of 41, each year of continuous employment entitles the employee to 1.5 weeks' pay.

However, an employee can only claim for 20 years' continuous employment and the weekly wage used in the calculation is capped by statute. At the time of writing the maximum weekly wage is £450. So the maximum basic award is £13,500 (20 years 1.5 £450).

✓ Make your answer stand out

Is the way in which these amounts are calculated consistent with the Employment Equality (Age) Regulations 2006, which are considered in the following chapter?

The basic award is not an award of damages and so the employee has no duty to mitigate the loss. However, the award can be reduced if the employee refuses an offer of reinstatement or re-engagement or if the employee's conduct makes a reduction equitable.

There can also be a *compensatory award* of up to £74,200. In cases where discrimination has occurred the amount of damages is unlimited. The compensatory award takes account of matters such as loss of earnings with no upper limit on the weekly pay, loss of statutory rights, loss of pension rights and a supplementary amount which can be awarded if the employer failed to go through an established appeals procedure. However, the employee has a duty to mitigate any losses and so would have to take another suitable job if one arose. The award will also be reduced by the amount of jobseeker's allowance which the applicant has received. Section 123(6) of the ERA 1996 allows the award to be reduced on the grounds of contributory negligence. For the purposes of the compensatory award the weekly pay received is the net pay rather than gross pay.

An additional award of between 13 and 26 weeks' pay can be made if the employer refuses to comply with a re-engagement or reinstatement order. If the dismissal was on the grounds of discrimination the additional award is of between 26 and 52 weeks' pay. As regards these awards the week's pay is still subject to the statutory maximum.

Wrongful dismissal

The dismissal must amount to a breach of contract by the employer. So there will be no **wrongful dismissal** if the employee's behaviour amounted to a breach of contract which would justify his or her dismissal.

KEY DEFINITION: Wrongful dismissal

Wrongful dismissal is the name given to a common law action for breach of contract, which arises when an employee is summarily dismissed, i.e. dismissed without the notice to which he or she was entitled.

REVISION NOTE

Remedies for breach of contract were considered in Chapter 4. The common law rules apply to cases of wrongful dismissal. So wrongful dismissal is quite unlike unfair dismissal, where the law is entirely statutory.

A term of the contract of employment generally sets out the notice which must be given. In addition, every employee is entitled to a reasonable amount of notice. Section 86 of the ERA 1996 sets out the following minimum notice periods:

Length of continuous employment	Notice entitlement
Less than 1 month	None
1 month–2 years	1 week
2 years–12 years	1 week per year worked
Over 12 years	12 weeks

Redundancy

KEY STATUTE

Employment Rights Act 1996, s. 139(1)

Section 139(1) of the ERA 1996 explains that an employee has been made redundant if he or she was dismissed wholly or mainly because:

- the employer ceased, or intended to cease, to carry on the business; or
- the employer ceased, or intended to cease, to carry on the business in the place where the employee was employed; or
- the need for work of a particular kind to be carried on, or to be carried on in the place where the employee worked, had either ceased or diminished or was expected to do so.

Dismissals for other reasons will not be redundancy but might be unfair or wrongful dismissal. Where the employer moves the place of business, whether or not the employees have been made redundant will depend upon the terms of the contract of employment, how far the business has moved and the amount of inconvenience caused to the employees by the move.

Who can claim redundancy?

In order to claim redundancy an employee must have at least two years' continuous employment since reaching the age of 18. People who are ordinarily employed outside Great Britain cannot claim.

Offer of suitable alternative employment

If the employer offers the employee suitable alternative employment, and the employee unreasonably refuses to accept this, then the employee cannot claim to have been made redundant. The offer of suitable alternative employment must be made within four weeks of the expiry of the employment and must be reasonable in all the circumstances.

Redundancy payments

A redundancy payment is calculated in the same manner as the basic award for unfair dismissal, but a redundancy payment cannot be reduced on account of the employee's conduct. As there is no compensatory award when a person is made redundant, many employees would receive a greater payment if they were unfairly dismissed rather than made redundant.

REVISION NOTE

The basic award for unfair dismissal was considered earlier in this chapter (see p. 159).

The terms of many contracts of employment agree that payments more generous than the statutory payments should be made in the event of redundancy.

Procedure

When a large number of people are to be made redundant, the following principles apply:

- The employer should give the employees as much warning as possible.
- The employer should consult the trade union in order to be fair and to cause as little hardship as possible.
- Subjective criteria should not be used. The process should be objective and matters such as attendance records and length of service should be considered.
- Union representatives should be consulted as to the appropriate criteria to be used.
- The employer should try to offer alternative employment instead of just making employees redundant.

If the employer does not follow these procedures then the employees will not have been made redundant but will have been unfairly dismissed. This could be beneficial to the employees as they might receive a compensatory award. As we have seen, the basic award for unfair dismissal will be the same as a statutory redundancy payment.

Consultation on redundancies

An employer who intends to make redundant 20 or more employees at one establishment, must consult with trade unions with a view to reaching agreement with them. If it is proposed to make at least 100 employees redundant at one establishment the Secretary of State must be notified in writing.

Putting it all together

Answer guidelines

See the essay question at the start of the chapter.

Approaching the question

- You will need to define unfair dismissal and redundancy and explain the ways in which they are different.
- You will also need to explain what is meant by unfair dismissal.
- Don't forget to give your opinion as to whether or not the quotation is true and to explain why it might be advantageous for an employer to claim that an unfairly dismissed employee was in fact made redundant.

Important points to include

- Explain the circumstances in which an employee is unfairly dismissed.
- Explain the grounds on which an employee can be made redundant.
- When considering why an employer might want to say that an unfairly dismissed employee was made redundant, you will need to explain the compensatory award which an unfairly dismissed employee might receive.
- Explain how an employee could be dismissed without having been unfairly dismissed or made redundant.

✓ Make your answer stand out

Structure your answer. Deal with each of the issues in turn and relate them to the quotation. The question asks you to explain that unfair dismissal and redundancy are not the same thing so you will need to explain the ways in which they are different. It also wants an explanation of dismissals which are not unfair. It would be a good idea to make up examples to show that you understand these matters. Don't forget to reach a conclusion!

READ TO IMPRESS

Harris, J. (2009) The Resolution to Workplace Disputes? 99(2) ELJ

Harwood, S. (2007) Unfair Dismissal, 31(17) CSR 131

Sanders, A. (2009) Part One of the Employment Act 2008: 'Better' Dispute Resolution? ILJ 30–49

Simpson, J. and Don, G. (2009) Constructive Dismissal: Once More Unto the Breach, 102(16) ELJ

www.pearsoned.co.uk/lawexpress

Go online to access more revision support including quizzes to test your knowledge, sample questions with answer guidelines, podcasts you can download, and more!

10 Employment 2: Discrimination

Revision checklist

Essential points you should know:

- ☐ The protected characteristics set out in the Equality Act 2010
- ☐ The types of discrimination outlawed by the Equality Act 2010
- ☐ The effect of the Part-time Workers (Prevention of Less Favourable Treatment) Regulations 2000, the Agency Workers Regulations 2010, the Fixed Term Employees (Prevention of Less Favourable Treatment) Regulations 2002 and the Rehabilitation of Offenders Act 1974

Topic map

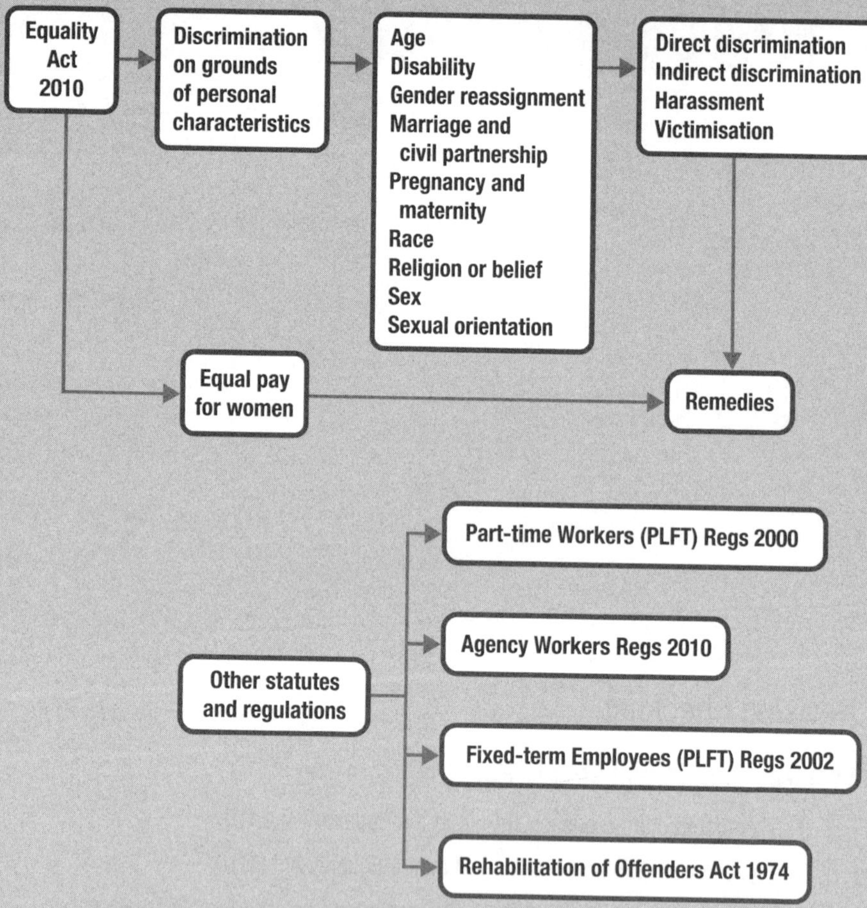

A printable version of this topic map is available from **www.pearsoned.co.uk/lawexpress**

Introduction

Exam questions are often asked on legislation which outlaws discrimination in employment.

This chapter begins by considering the Equality Act 2010 which has consolidated the law on discrimination based on a **personal characteristic**. The Equality Act has replaced important statutes such as the Equal Pay Act 1970, the Sex Discrimination Act 1975 and the Race Relations Act 1976. The chapter concludes by looking at the protection given to part-time employees, agency workers, employees on **fixed-term contracts** and people with criminal records.

ASSESSMENT ADVICE

Essay questions

As well as asking you to describe the effect of anti-discrimination legislation, many questions will ask for your opinion on some aspect of the legislation. If a question does ask for an opinion, make sure that you give an opinion and that you justify it by reference to the relevant legislation.

Problem questions

Read the question. Does it require you to consider just one piece of legislation or several? If it concerns equal pay for women, explain that the approach taken is not the same as the approach taken to a question which concerns direct discrimination, indirect discrimination, victimisation or harassment on the grounds of a personal characteristic.

Sample question

Could you answer this question? Below is a typical problem question that could arise on this topic. Guidelines on answering the question are included at the end of this chapter, while a sample essay question and guidance on tackling it can be found on the companion website.

PROBLEM QUESTION

Taxi Ltd is a company which employs 60 taxi drivers. Some taxi drivers are promoted to the position of taxi planner. The taxi planners take calls and allocate drivers to those calls.

They are paid about 20% more per hour than taxi drivers. Avril was the only female taxi driver to have been promoted to the position of taxi planner. She left the job altogether soon afterwards because the general office manager continuously made sexual innuendos about her. Belle applied to replace Avril but was told that the job of office planner was no longer open to women because they spoilt the atmosphere in the taxi planners' office. Charles, who works only ten hours a week, is paid a lower hourly rate than other taxi drivers on the grounds that he earns enough to live on in his other job as a butcher.

Advise Taxi Ltd of its legal position in respect of Avril, Belle and Charles.

Equality Act 2010: Discrimination on grounds of personal characteristics

The Equality Act 2010 outlaws direct discrimination, indirect discrimination victimisation and harassment on the grounds of one or more personal characteristics.

KEY DEFINITION: Personal characteristics

Section 4 of the Act lists the nine personal characteristics on account of which discrimination is not allowed. These characteristics are:

- age;
- disability;
- gender reassignment;
- marriage and civil partnership;
- pregnancy and maternity;
- race (including colour, nationality, or ethnic or national origins);
- religion or belief;
- sex; and
- sexual orientation

KEY CASE

***Mandla* v. *Dowell Lee* [1983] 1 All ER 1062 (HL)**

Concerning: what is an ethnic group?

Facts

The facts of this case are lengthy and complicated and to summarise them here would add little to an understanding of the legal principle outlined below. Remember that examiners are usually looking for an understanding of the *ratio* and legal principle and that reciting the facts in an exam will not improve your grade.

Legal principle

The House of Lords held that an ethnic group must have two essential characteristics and that another five characteristics would commonly be found. The two essential characteristics of ethnic groups are:

1. the group has a long shared history of which it is conscious as distinguishing it from other groups and the memory of which it keeps alive; and
2. the group has a cultural tradition of its own, including family and social customs and manners, which is often but not necessarily associated with religious observance.

The five non-essential characteristics are:

(a) common origin from one geographical area or descent from a small number of ancestors;

(b) a common language, even though others might speak it;

(c) a common literature which is peculiar to the group;

(d) a common religion which is different from that of neighbouring groups or that of the general surrounding community;

(e) being a minority or being an oppressed or dominant group within a larger community.

A person who is claiming discrimination will need to prove that, on account of one of the listed personal characteristics he or she suffered **direct discrimination**, indirect discrimination, victimisation or harassment.

Direct discrimination

KEY DEFINITION: Direct discrimination

Section 13(1) provides that a person (A) discriminates against another (B) if, because of a protected characteristic A treats B less favourably than A treats or would treat others.

For example, an employer would commit direct discrimination if he or she refused to employ a person because he or she was a Muslim.

Indirect discrimination

KEY STATUTE

Equality Act 2010, s. 19(1)

Section 19(1) provides that a person (A) discriminates against another (B) if A applies to B a provision, criterion or practice which is discriminatory in relation to a protected characteristic of B's (except pregnancy and maternity). A provision, criterion or practice is discriminatory in relation to a protected characteristic of B's if:

- A applies it, or would apply it, to persons with whom B does not share the characteristic;
- it puts, or would put, persons with whom B shares the characteristic at a particular disadvantage when compared with persons with whom B does not share it;
- it puts, or would put, B at that disadvantage; *and*
- A cannot show it to be a proportionate way of achieving a legitimate aim.

So it might be indirect discrimination if an employer imposed a new shift pattern on all employees and this new pattern prevented women with young children from continuing in the job.

If direct or indirect discrimination is alleged, s. 23 provides that the person making the allegation must do so by reference to a **comparator**. The comparator can be a real or hypothetical person whose circumstances are the same as the claimant's, except that the comparator does not share the claimant's protected characteristic.

Victimisation

Section 27(1) provides that a person (A) victimises another (B) if A subjects B to a detriment because B has either done a protected act or A believes that B has done, or may do, a protected act. A protected act would include bringing proceedings under the Act or doing anything else in connection with the Act.

Harassment

KEY STATUTE

Equality Act, s. 26(1) The meaning of harassment

Section 26(1) provides that a person (A) harasses another (B) if:

(a) A engages in unwanted conduct related to a relevant protected characteristic, or of a sexual nature, and:

(b) the conduct has the effect of

(i) violating B's dignity; or

(ii) creating an intimidating, hostile, degrading, humiliating or offensive environment for B.

Discrimination in the employment field

Section 39 states that when selecting employees it is unlawful to discriminate against another:

- by making discriminatory arrangements for the purposes of determining who should be offered employment; or
- by offering discriminatory terms of employment; or
- by refusing or deliberately omitting to offer employment.
- As regards existing employees, it is unlawful to discriminate:
- in the terms of the employment;
- in the way in which access to opportunities for promotion, transfer or training, or to any other benefits are given; or by refusing or deliberately omitting to allow access to these things; or
- by dismissing the employee or subjecting him or her to any other detriment.

Permissible discrimination

Schedule 9 provides a defence of occupational requirement to an employer who refuses to offer someone a job, or dismisses them or refuses to offer them promotion, etc. The employer will have to show that, having regard to the nature or context of the work, a requirement imposed by the employer is an occupational requirement which the employee or applicant for the job does not have. The employer will also need to show that it is a proportionate means of achieving a legitimate aim.

Figure 10.1

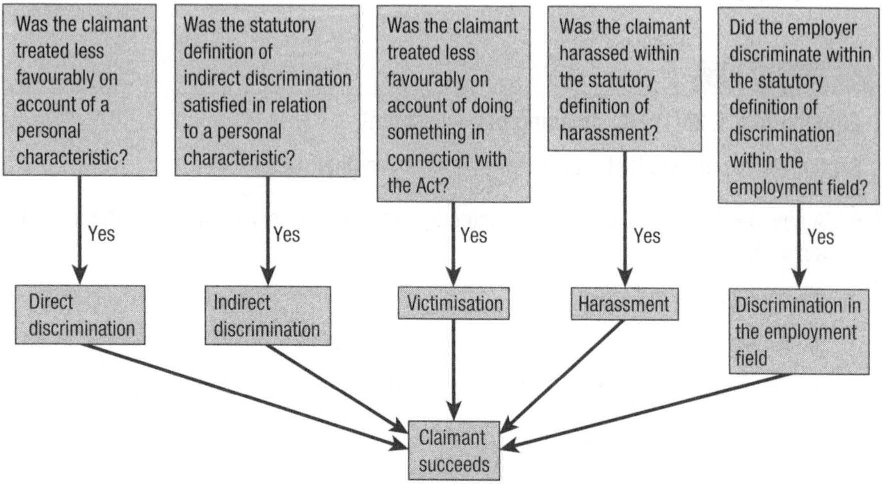

Figure 10.1 shows how to approach discrimination on the grounds of a personal characteristic.

Equality Act 2010: Equal pay and conditions for women

The Equality Act 2010 requires that men and women who work for the same employer should be treated equally as regards pay and other benefits. A man can bring a claim but it is generally women who do so. It is therefore convenient to talk of a claim as being brought by a woman. In order to bring a claim, a woman will need to find a male **comparator** with whom she wishes to compare herself. The comparator must work for the same employer or for an associated employer.

A woman can bring a claim on three grounds:

1. that she does **like work** with that of the comparator;
2. that the work she does is rated as equivalent to that of the comparator; or
3. that the work she does is of equal value to that done by the comparator.

KEY DEFINITION: Like work

Section 65(1) provides that a woman does like work with that of a man if her work is broadly similar to that of the man. Any difference between what she does and what the man does must not be of practical importance in relation to the terms and conditions of employment.

! Don't be tempted to . . .

You should not think that it is always easy to say whether work is broadly similar in nature. Local authorities have recently conducted a massive pay equalisation scheme. Refuse workers, who are nearly always male, have been compared with carers, who are largely female. Can such a comparison validly be made?

Work will be rated as equivalent only if a properly conducted job evaluation scheme has found that the work is equivalent. Work done by a woman will be of equal value to that of a male comparator if the demands made on the woman are comparable with the demands made on the male, taking into account matters such as effort, skill and decision-making.

A defence is available if the employer can prove that the different treatment complained of was due to a genuine material factor such as qualifications or responsibility allowances.

Equal pay remedies

KEY STATUTE

Equality Act, s. 66(1)

If a woman proves that she does like work, work rated as equivalent or work which is of equal value to that of a male comparator, s. 66(1) of the EA 2010 provides that the woman's contract of employment should be deemed to include an *equality clause*. This clause would require all of the terms of the woman's contract to be changed so that they become no less favourable than similar terms in the male comparator's contract. The woman's contract should also be changed so that it includes any beneficial term in the male comparator's contract.

Article 157 of the Treaty on the Functioning of the European Union requires member states of the EU to ensure the application of the principle of equal pay for male and female workers if they do equal work, or work of equal value. In *Pickstone* v. *Freeman* plc (1988) the House of Lords indicated that national courts should try to interpret equal pay legislation so as to give effect to what is now Article 157.

REVISION NOTE

In Chapter 11 the effect of EU law is explained.

KEY CASE

***Birmingham City Council* v. *Abdulla* [2012] UKSC 47**

Concerning: the right to make equal pay claims in the county court

Facts

The facts of this case are lengthy and complicated and to summarise them here would add little to an understanding of the legal principle outlined below.

Legal principle

The Supreme Court held that a person bringing an equal pay claim can do so in the county court instead of before an employment tribunal. This is very significant because a claim for equal pay can be brought in the county court while still in the employment or within six years of leaving it. A claim for equal pay must be brought before an employment tribunal while still in the employment or within six months of leaving it.

Both damages and up to six years' back-pay can be awarded. Section 66(1) and Article 157 are not limited to wages or salary. Terms dealing with matters such as redundancy payments, payments for attending courses, travel benefits for retired employees and sick pay have all been held to be within the meaning of the Act.

✓ **Make your answer stand out**

Despite equal pay legislation having been in force for 40 years, women are, on average, paid significantly less than men. When answering an appropriate question you might consider why this should be so and whether women are likely to become more highly paid than men.

Enforcement and remedies in cases of discrimination

A complaint of personal characteristic discrimination must be brought to an employment tribunal within three months of the act complained of. A conciliation officer then attempts conciliation and only if this fails will the case reach the employment tribunal. If the complainant proves facts which could, in the absence of explanation, lead the tribunal to conclude that there has been an unlawful act of discrimination, then the employer will be liable unless he or she can prove that he or she did not commit the act in question.

The tribunal may:

- make an order declaring the complainant's right; or
- order the payment of damages; or
- order the employer to take action to prevent the effect of the discrimination.

There is no upper limit on the amount of damages, which can take account of injured feelings. The Commission for Equality and Human Rights can issue non-discrimination notices and can bring cases to court even where there has been no personal complaint.

Discrimination against part-time workers

The Part-time Workers (Prevention of Less Favourable Treatment) Regulations 2000 outlaw discrimination against part-time workers. These regulations do not take the same approach as the Equality Act 2010. Discrimination is prohibited only if the work done by the part-time employee is the 'same or broadly similar' to the work done by a full-time employee.

KEY CASE

***Matthews and Others* v. *Kent and Medway Towns Fire Authority* [2006] UKHL 8 (HL)**

Concerning: the approach to the Part-time Workers (PLFT) Regs 2000

Facts

The facts of this case are lengthy and complicated and to summarise them here would add little to an understanding of the legal principle outlined below.

Legal principle

The correct approach to the Regulations is to concentrate on similarities between the work done by both groups. It did not matter that the full-timers had additional duties. The approach is not the same as the one used under the Equality Act 2010 because it is inevitable that part-time work is in some ways different from full-time work.

The **pro rata principle** is used to assess whether or not a part-time worker has been treated less favourably.

KEY DEFINITION: Pro rata principle

The pro rata principle requires that a part-time worker should receive the appropriate proportion of pay and other benefits enjoyed by a full-time worker with whom he or she compares him- or herself.

These benefits include sick pay, maternity pay, access to pension schemes, training, career breaks and holiday entitlement. A part-timer is not entitled to overtime rates until working longer than full-time hours.

Figure 10.2 shows the effect in outline of the Part-time Workers Regulations 2000.

Figure 10.2

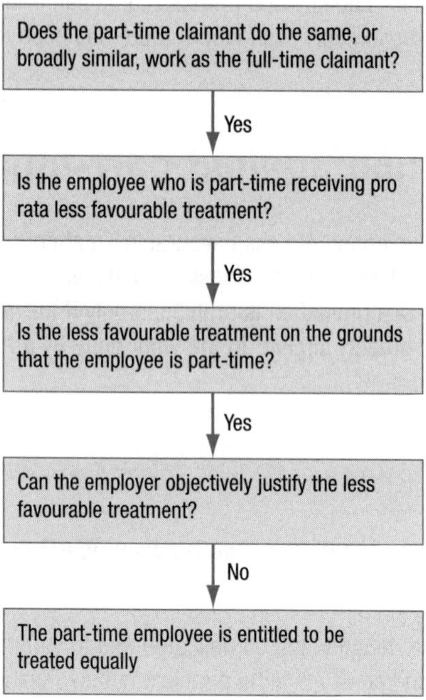

Agency workers

The Agency Workers Regulations 2010 give **agency workers** the same rights as workers employed directly by the employer, but only as regards six matters, known as the 'relevant terms and conditions'. These relevant terms and conditions are: pay, the duration of working time, night work, rest periods, rest breaks and annual leave.

KEY DEFINITION: Agency worker

Regulation 3 defines an agency worker as an individual who is supplied by a temporary work agency to work temporarily for and under the direct supervision of a hirer. The worker must have a contract of employment with the agency and self-employed people who provide services for an agency are not included.

REVISION NOTE

The difference between being an employee and being an independent contractor was considered at the beginning of Chapter 9.

Fixed-term workers

The Fixed-term Employees (Prevention of Less Favourable Treatment) Regulations 2002 provide that workers on **fixed-term contracts** should not be treated less favourably than other workers, unless there is a justifiable reason for the less favourable treatment.

KEY DEFINITION: Fixed-term contract

A contract is a fixed-term contract if it is agreed at the outset that it will exist for a fixed time, rather than being a contract which can be ended by giving notice.

In order to claim, a comparator working for the same employer must be found.

Persons with criminal records

The Rehabilitation of Offenders Act 1974 allows people whose convictions have become *spent* to deny that they have ever been convicted. Furthermore, if a person is dismissed because of a spent conviction this will amount to unfair dismissal.

Some criminal offences involving children are never spent. Otherwise, a conviction becomes spent after a length of time which varies with the severity of the sentence passed. The times are as follows:

Over 2.5 years' imprisonment	Never spent
6 months–2.5 years	Spent after 10 years
Less than 6 months	Spent after 7 years
Fine	Spent after 5 years
Community Service Order	Spent after 5 years
Probation/Binding Over	Spent after 5 years
Conditional discharge	Spent after 1 year
Care/Supervision order	Spent after 1 year
Absolute discharge	Spent after 6 months

Putting it all together

Answer guidelines

See the problem question at the start of the chapter.

Approaching the question

It looks as though unlawful discrimination has occurred, and you will need to apply the correct legislation accurately.

Important points to include

- Consider Avril and Belle separately.
- Has either employee been illegally discriminated against?
- In what way (direct, indirect, etc.) did the discrimination occur?
- Was the discrimination permissible?
- What remedies might be available?
- What will Charles need to prove?

✓ Make your answer stand out

Go through the relevant legislation thoroughly, dealing with each requirement in turn. Make sure that you reach a conclusion.

READ TO IMPRESS

Fredman, S. (1977) Reversing Discrimination, 113 LQR 575

McCrudden, C. (1986) Rethinking Positive Action, 15 ILJ 219

Swift, J. (2006) Justifying Age Discrimination, 35 ILJ 228

www.pearsoned.co.uk/lawexpress

Go online to access more revision support including quizzes to test your knowledge, sample questions with answer guidelines, podcasts you can download, and more!

11

Sources of English law

Revision checklist

Essential points you should know:

- [ ] The main sources of English law
- [ ] How legislation is made and interpreted
- [ ] The way in which the system of judicial precedent operates
- [ ] The effect of European law on English law
- [ ] The impact of the Human Rights Act 1998

Topic map

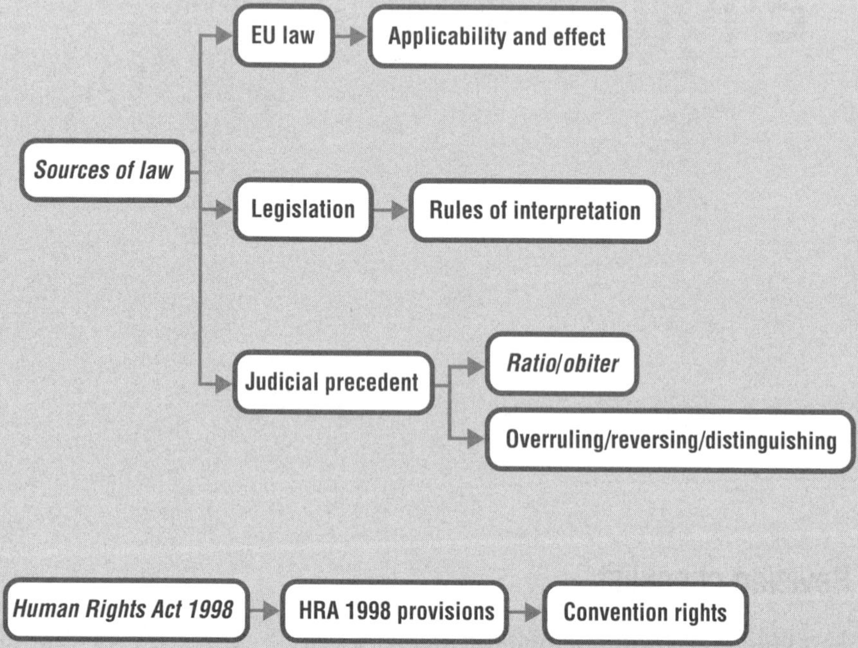

A printable version of this topic map is available from **www.pearsoned.co.uk/lawexpress**

Introduction

The decisions of higher-ranking courts must be followed by lower-ranking courts.

An understanding of the sources of English law is essential if a legal exam question is to be answered well. There are three major sources of English law:

1. legislation;
2. judicial precedent; and
3. European Union law.

The Human Rights Act 1998 is not a source of law in its own right but it has a significant effect on the way in which courts interpret and apply the law.

ASSESSMENT ADVICE

Problem questions

Problem questions on sources of law are not common. But an understanding of the relative strengths of the various sources of law allows problem questions to be answered in depth. When answering such a question you will gain good marks for showing, for example, that a decision of the Supreme Court is of much more authority than a decision of the High Court.

Sample question

Could you answer this question? Below is a typical essay question that could arise on this topic. Guidelines on answering the question are included at the end of this chapter. Another sample question and guidance on tackling it can be found on the companion website.

ESSAY QUESTION

Stevenson v. *Rogers* (set out on p. 27) was decided in the Court of Appeal. State what you consider the *ratio decidendi* of the case might be, and explain how the ratio of a case differs from *obiter dicta*. Explain also the extent to which other courts would be bound by *Stevenson* v. *Rogers* and how the case could be overruled or distinguished.

Guidelines on answering this question are included at the end of this chapter.

Legislation

Legislation is the name given to statutes and delegated legislation passed by the UK Parliament. Statutes, as Acts of Parliament are known, become law after they have passed through both Houses of Parliament and gained the Royal Assent. Delegated legislation, which often takes the form of regulations, is passed using a modified procedure. Legislation is the ultimate source of law and the UK Parliament has the power, in theory at least, to pass any statute it wants to.

Rules of statutory interpretation

There are three main rules of statutory interpretation: the **literal rule**, the **golden rule** and the **mischief rule**. These rules are also applied when a court interprets delegated legislation.

KEY DEFINITION: Literal, golden, and mischief rule

The literal rule, also known as the literal approach, holds that the words of a statute should be given their ordinary, grammatical meaning even if this produces an absurd result.

The golden rule, also known as the purposive approach, holds that the words of a statute should be given their ordinary, grammatical meaning as far as possible but not if this would produce an absurd result.

The mischief rule allows the court to consider what mischief, or problem, the statute was passed to correct.

The landmark case *Pepper* v. *Hart* (1993) held that the debates in Parliament can be looked at, in very limited circumstances, if this is the only way to resolve an ambiguity in legislation.

Judicial precedent

The doctrine of judicial precedent holds that the decisions of superior courts are binding upon inferior courts. So when a superior court reaches a decision it is creating law because that decision will later have to be followed by all courts below it in the hierarchy. Figure 11.1 shows the hierarchy of the courts and which courts bind which other courts.

Figure 11.1

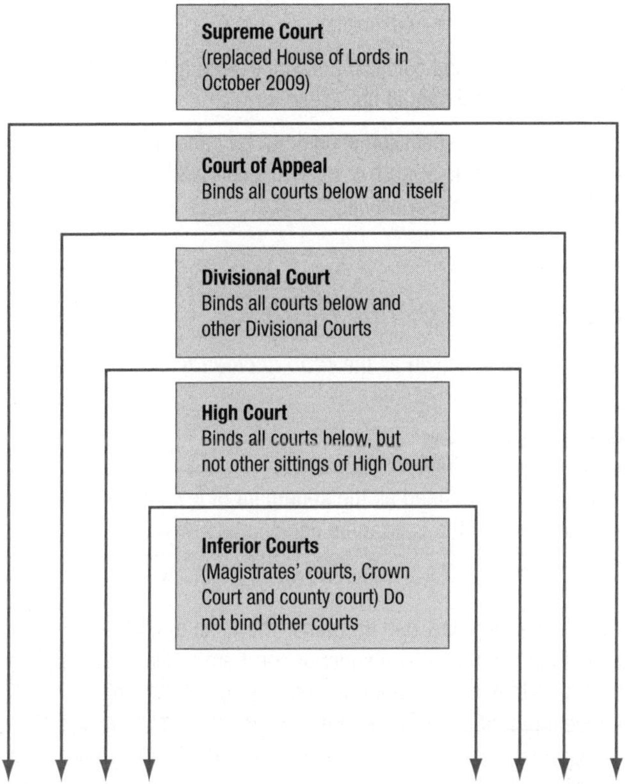

KEY CASE

***Young* v. *Bristol Aeroplane Co Ltd* [1944] KB 718 (CA)**

Concerning: the circumstances in which the Court of Appeal is not bound by its own previous decisions

Facts

The facts of this case are lengthy and complicated and to summarise them here would add little to an understanding of the legal principle outlined below. Remember that examiners are usually looking for an understanding of the *ratio* and legal principle and that reciting the facts in an exam will not improve your grade.

Legal principle

The Court of Appeal can refuse to follow its own previous decisions in only three circumstances:

1. where there are two conflicting earlier Court of Appeal decisions, it can decide which one to follow and which one to overrule;
2. if a previous Court of Appeal decision has since been overruled by the Supreme Court, the Court of Appeal should not follow it;
3. a previous Court of Appeal decision should not be followed if it was decided through lack of care, ignoring some statute or other higher-ranking authority such as a previously decided Supreme Court case.

Ratio decidendi and *obiter dicta*

The binding part of a case is known as the ***ratio decidendi*** (the reason for the decision).

KEY DEFINITION: Ratio decidendi

The *ratio decidendi* can be defined as the statement of law which the court applied to the facts and which caused the case to be decided as it was.

Notice that only statements of law can be *ratios*. The facts of a case are never the *ratio* of it. Not all statements of law made by a superior court are ratios. Some statements of law are **obiter dicta** (other things said). Although *obiters* are not binding on any courts they can be persuasive, meaning that other courts are likely to follow them unless there is a good reason not to. A court which makes a precedent does not state what the *ratio* of the case is. It is other courts which later decide what the *ratio* is when they are deciding whether or not to follow the case.

! Don't be tempted to . . .

You should not think that it is always easy to say what the *ratio decidendi* of a case is. Judges do not say what they consider to be the *ratio* of cases which they decide. A great deal of legal argument involves opposing views as to what constitutes the *ratio* of a particular case.

Overruling, reversing and distinguishing

A higher court, or a statute, can overrule an existing *ratio*. When this happens, the case in which the overruled *ratio* was made is named, declared to be wrong and then treated as if it had never been a precedent.

Overruling is not the same as reversing. When a case is reversed, all that happens is that the party who appealed the decision of a lower court wins the appeal. So the appeal court merely reverses the outcome of the case. Generally, no new precedent is created.

When a case is distinguished a lower court refuses to follow a decision which appears to be binding. It does this on the grounds that the facts of the case are so materially different from the facts of the case in which the precedent was made that it would be inappropriate to follow the precedent.

Partridge v. *Crittenden* (1968), a case considered in Chapter 1 (on p. 5), can be used to demonstrate the terms explained above. The *ratio* of the case might be that newspaper advertisements which state the price at which goods can be bought are generally invitations to treat rather than offers. As the case was decided in the Divisional Court, it would be binding on lower courts such as the Crown Court and the magistrates' court. A higher court, such as the Supreme Court, could overrule it. In *Partridge* v. *Crittenden*, the Divisional Court did in fact reverse the decision of the magistrates' court from which the appeal was made. The magistrates had found the defendant guilty whereas the Divisional Court found him not guilty. Any court could distinguish *Partridge* v. *Crittenden* if it found the ratio inapplicable to the case in front of it. If a lower court distinguished the case it could refuse to follow it. Several *obiters* were made in *Partridge* v. *Crittenden*, such as the statement that if the defendant had been charged with the separate offence of selling a wild bird, he would have been guilty of that offence.

> ✓ Make your answer stand out
>
> Judicial precedent makes up the majority of English law. In an appropriate question you should consider whether it is appropriate for the judges to make the law. Are the judges representative of society as a whole? Could a representative sample of society as a whole make the law as well as the precedent-making judges?

European Union law

The European Communities Act 1972 provides that the United Kingdom will apply EU law in United Kingdom courts and that if there is any conflict between EU law and UK domestic law then EU law will prevail. So UK statutes have to be interpreted in a way that is consistent with EU law.

The primary legislation of the EU consists of the articles of the Treaty on the Functioning of the European Union. There are over 300 articles and some, such as Article 157 which outlaws sex discrimination, are of much more importance than others.

The secondary legislation of the EC consists of regulations, directives and decisions.

Regulations, which often deal with fairly technical matters, are directly applicable in all member states without the approval of the parliaments of those states.

Directives are not immediately binding, but require member states to pass legislation to bring them into effect by the time of their implementation date. The UK generally implements directives by passing delegated legislation, such as the Unfair Terms in Consumer Contracts Regulations 1999. However, the United Kingdom Parliament has also passed several important statutes, such as the Consumer Protection Act 1987, in order to implement directives. Even after the UK has passed legislation to implement a directive the European Court can apply the directive and the UK courts must take account of such decisions.

Decisions are immediately binding, but only on those to whom they are addressed, usually member governments or corporations.

Recommendations and opinions can also be made by the European Commission. These do not have any binding legal force. However, if a member state passes legislation to comply with a recommendation or a decision, any national court can refer a case to the European Court of Justice to see whether or not it applies and how it should be interpreted.

Applicability and effect

EU legislation is *directly applicable* if it automatically forms part of the domestic law of member states. Treaty articles are always directly applicable, as are EU regulations. But a claimant could only rely on the legislation in a UK court if it was capable of having *direct effect*. Where EU legislation has direct effect an individual can directly rely upon the legislation, either to sue or as a defence, in the domestic courts of his or her country. No EU legislation can have direct effect unless it is sufficiently clear, precise and unconditional. Many Treaty articles do not meet these requirements as they are mere statements of intention.

Even if EC legislation does have direct effect, it may have only direct *vertical* effect, rather than direct *horizontal* effect. If it has direct vertical effect it can be used by an individual only against the state and against emanations of the state, such as health authorities. This is called vertical effect because the state is regarded as above the individual. If it has direct horizontal effect it can also be used by one individual against another individual. This is called horizontal effect because the individuals are regarded as being on the same level as each other.

REVISION NOTE

In the previous chapter we saw that Article 157 of the EC Treaty requires member states of the EU to ensure application of the principle of equal pay for male and female workers if they do equal work, or work of equal value. You can use this as an example of how EC law has a major impact on English law.

Human Rights Act 1998

The European Convention on Human Rights was drawn up in 1950. The UK *ratified* the Convention in 1951. The Human Rights Act 1998 has significantly increased the importance of the rights contained in the Convention.

KEY STATUTE

Human Rights Act 1998, s. 2

Section 2 of the HRA 1998 requires any court or tribunal which is considering a question which has arisen in connection with a Convention right to take into account any decision of the European Court of Human Rights.

The European Court of Human Rights sits in Strasbourg and is quite separate from the European Court of Justice, which sits in Luxembourg. The European Court of Human Rights is very much a court of last resort. Article 35 of the Convention requires an applicant to the court to prove four things:

1. that the complaint involves a breach of the Convention by a country which has ratified it;
2. that the breach happened within that country's jurisdiction;
3. that all domestic remedies have been exhausted; *and*
4. the application has been made within six months of these being exhausted.

Section 3 of the HRA 1998 requires that all legislation is read and given effect in a way which is compatible with the Convention rights, but only in so far as it is possible to do this. Any precedent-making court has the power in any legal proceedings to make a declaration of incompatibility, stating that any legislation is incompatible with Convention rights. But this would not invalidate the legislation in question. It would give the relevant minister the option to revoke or amend the legislation. Any court can declare delegated legislation, but not statutes, invalid on the grounds of incompatibility. However, this is not the case if the parent Act, which gave authority for the delegated legislation in question to be passed, provides that the legislation should prevail even if it is incompatible.

KEY STATUTE

Human Rights Act 1998, s. 6(1)

Section 6(1) of the HRA 1998 provides that it is unlawful for a public authority to act in a way which is inconsistent with a Convention right, unless the public authority could not have acted differently as a result of a UK Act of Parliament.

If a public authority breaches a Convention right, a victim of the breach may bring legal proceedings against it for breach of a new public tort.

Whenever a new Bill is introduced into Parliament, s. 19 of the HRA 1998 says that the relevant minister must make a statement to Parliament, before the second reading, declaring that the legislation either is compatible or is not. If the minister states that the legislation is incompatible he or she must state that the government intends to proceed with it anyway. The minister does not need to state the way in which the legislation is incompatible.

The rights conferred by the Convention are as follows:

- the right to life (Article 2);
- the right not to be subjected to torture or inhumane or degrading punishment (Article 3);
- the right not to be held in slavery or servitude or required to perform forced or compulsory labour (Article 4);
- the right to liberty and security of the person (Article 5);
- the right to a fair trial (Article 6);
- the right not to be convicted of a criminal offence which was created after the act was committed (Article 7);
- the right to respect for a person's private and family life, home and correspondence (Article 8);
- the right to freedom of thought, conscience and religion (Article 9);
- the right to freedom of expression (Article 10);
- the right to freedom of peaceful assembly and to freedom of association with others (Article 11);
- the right to marry and form a family (Article 12);
- the right to an effective remedy for violation of the rights and freedoms set out in the Convention (Article 13);
- the right to have the Convention applied without discrimination (Article 14).

The UK has also agreed to be bound by two protocols. One of these gives the right to peaceful enjoyment of possessions; the other outlaws the death penalty.

Article 15 allows departure from the Convention in time of war.

EXAM TIP

Use Figure 11.2 to structure an answer on the HRA 1998.

Figure 11.2

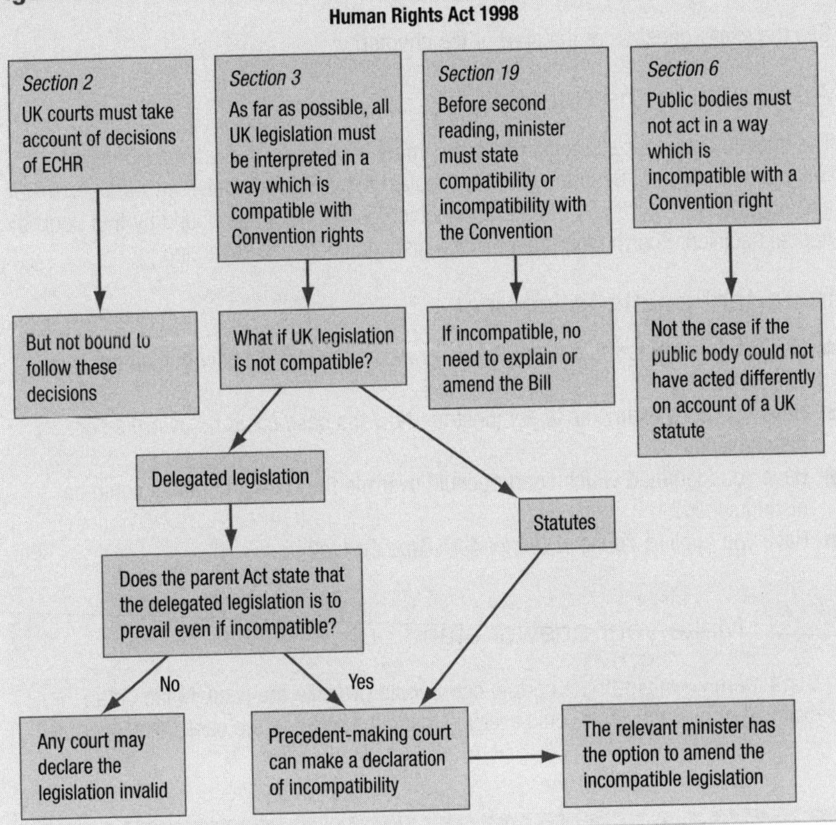

Putting it all together

Answer guidelines

See the essay question at the start of the chapter.

Approaching the question

The question has four elements. First, you must try to state the *ratio decidendi* of *Stevenson* v. *Rogers*. Second, you must explain the difference between *ratio decidendi* and *obiter dicta*. Third, you must explain which courts would be bound by this Court of Appeal decision. Fourth, you must explain distinguishing and reversing.

Important points to include

- Have you attempted to state a possible *ratio* and explained how this differs from *obiter dicta*?
- Have you used examples to demonstrate how the case could be overruled or distinguished?
- Have you identified which court(s) could overrule the case and how it could be distinguished?
- Have you applied *Young* v. *Bristol Aeroplane Co Ltd*?

✓ Make your answer stand out

Don't merely explain that a certain court could overrule the case. Make up an example of how the court could overrule it and the effect of the case being overruled.

READ TO IMPRESS

Clayton, R. (2007) The Human Rights Act Six Years On: Where Are We Now? EHRLR 11

Ewing, K. (2004) The Futility of the Human Rights Act, PL 249

Gearty, C. (2002) Reconciling Parliamentary Democracy and Human Rights, LQR 248

Lester, A. (2005) The Utility of the Human Rights Act: A Reply to Keith Ewing, PL 249

And finally, before the exam . . .

This book will have given you a good overall understanding of business law. You should be ready for the exam and be looking forward to it. Remember to take your time with problem questions. Do not start writing until you have clearly identified the relevant issues. Having identified the issues, state the relevant principles of law and apply them to the question. Make sure that your answers to both problem and essay questions show that you have a good, basic knowledge of all of the topics which your business law course covers. Make sure too that you apply the law to the question which has been set.

Test yourself

- ☐ Look at the **revision checklists** at the start of each chapter. Are you happy that you can now tick them all? If not, go back to the particular chapter and work through the material again. If you are still struggling, seek help from your tutor.
- ☐ Attempt to answer the **sample questions** in each chapter and check your answers against the guidelines provided.
- ☐ Go online to **www.pearsoned.co.uk/lawexpress** for more hands-on revision help and try out these resources:
  - ☐ Try the **test your knowledge** quizzes and see if you can score full marks for each chapter.
  - ☐ Attempt to answer the **sample questions** for each chapter within the time limit and check your answers against the guidelines provided.
  - ☐ Listen to the **podcast** and then attempt the question it discusses.
  - ☐ **'You be the marker'** and see if you can spot the strengths and weaknesses of the sample answers.
  - ☐ Use the **flashcards** to test your recall of the legal principles of the cases and statutes you've revised and the definitions of important terms. ▶

- [ ] Make sure that you know the difference between **contractual** and **tortious** liability.
- [ ] Make sure that you know the different legal rules which apply to **companies**, **partnerships** and **limited liability partnerships**.
- [ ] Check that you know the various **employment rights** and the ways in which **discrimination** in employment is outlawed.

Linking it all up

Do not forget that all of the chapters in this book are interrelated. The law of contract, for example, is not just a subject in its own right. The law of employment and the law relating to partnerships, limited liability partnerships and companies are all based on the law of contract. Check where there are overlaps between subject areas. (You may want to review the 'revision note' boxes throughout this book.) Make a careful note of these as knowing how one topic may lead into another can increase your marks significantly. Here are some examples:

✔ Contract of employment is created in the same way as other contracts.

✔ Companies, partners and LLPs can be liable in either contract or tort.

✔ An understanding of the sources of law will improve an exam answer on any legal topic.

Knowing your cases

Make sure you know how to use relevant case law in your answers. Use the table below to focus your revision of the key cases in each topic. To review the details of these cases, refer back to the particular chapter.

Key case	How to use	Related topics
Chapter 1 Formation of a contract		
Partridge v. *Crittenden*	To show that most advertisements are invitations to treat	Offers and invitations to treat distinguished

Key case	How to use	Related topics
Carlill v. *The Carbolic* Smoke Ball Co. Ltd	To show that some advertisements can make a unilateral offer to the whole world	Offers and invitations to treat distinguished
Holwell Securities Ltd v. *Hughes*	To show the limitations of the postal rule	Offer, acceptance and revocation
The High Trees case	To set out the requirements of promissory estoppel	The need for consideration
Chapter 2 The terms of the contract		
The Hong Kong Fir Shipping case	To show the effect of an innominate term	Conditions, warranties and innominate terms
Bramhill v. *Edwards*	To show the meaning of satisfactory quality	Objectivity and the reasonable man
Chapter 3 Misrepresentation, mistake, duress, illegality, minors and privity		
Car and Universal Finance Ltd v. *Caldwell*	To show how a voidable contract can be avoided	Misrepresentation, mistake, duress and undue influence
Bell v. *Lever Bros Ltd*	To show the limits on mistake as to quality	
Cundy v. *Lindsay*	To show when mistake as to the person can make a contract void	Misrepresentation
King's Norton Metal Co. Ltd v. *Edridge Merrett & Co. Ltd*	To show when mistake as to the person cannot make a contract void	Misrepresentation
Saunders v. *Anglia Building Society*	To show the limits of non est factum	
Chapter 4 Discharge of contractual obligations and remedies		
Krell v. *Henry*	To show the circumstances in which a contract can be frustrated	

Key case	How to use	Related topics
Herne Bay Steamboat Co. v. *Hutton*	To show the limits on frustration	
Maritime National Fish Ltd v. *Ocean Trawlers Ltd*	To show the limits on frustration	
Victoria Laundry Ltd v. *Newman Industries Ltd*	To demonstrate the application of the two rules in *Hadley* v. *Baxendale*	Breach of contract of a sale of goods
Chapter 5 Tort		
Donoghue v. *Stevenson*	To show the requirements of the tort of negligence	Occupiers liability
Caparo Industries plc v. *Dickman*	To show the limits on extending a duty of care to new situations	
Hedley Byrne & Co Lyd v. *Heller and Partners Ltd*	To show the requirements of negligent misstatement	Negligent misrepresentation
Chapter 6 Companies 1: Formation and personnel		
Salomon v. *Salomon & Co Ltd*	To show that a company has a separate legal identity of its own	Companies, partnerships and LLPs
Panorama Developments v. *Fidelis Furnishing Fabrics Ltd*	To show the extent to which a company secretary can act as agent of the company	Company directors
Chapter 7 Companies 2: Shares, resolutions, protection of minority shareholders and charges		
Re Yorkshire Woolcombers Association Ltd	To show the nature of a floating charge	Fixed and floating charges
Chapter 8 Partnership, limited liability partnership and sole trading		
No relevant cases		

Key case	How to use	Related topics
Chapter 9 Employment 1: Contract, rights, dismissal and redundancy		
No relevant cases		
Chapter 10 Employment 2: Discrimination		
Mandla v. *Dowell Lee*	To show the meaning of ethnic group	
Birmingham City Council v. *Abdulla*	To extend the time limit for an equal pay claim	
Matthews v. *Kent and Medway Towns Fire Authority*	To show how the Part-time Workers Regulations should be applied	
Chapter 11 Sources of English Law		
Young v. Bristol Aeroplance Co. Ltd	To show when the Court of Appeal can refuse to follow one of its own precedents	

Sample question

Below is an essay question that incorporates overlapping areas of the law. See if you can answer this question drawing upon your knowledge of the whole subject area. Guidelines on answering this question are included at the end of this section.

ESSAY QUESTION

The law now adequately protects consumers, minority shareholders and employees. It is no longer possible for businesses to ignore their rights and their legitimate expectations.

To what extent do you agree with the above statement?

Answer guidelines

Approaching the question

This question refers to the legal protection given to three different groups of people: consumers, minority shareholders and employees. You will need to consider the law in relation to each of these three groups. Also, in relation to the three groups, you will need to say whether or not you agree with the statement in the question. However, you must make sure that your opinion is given in the light of the legal protection which currently exists. A mere opinion which does not refer to the legal position will not be answering the question.

Important points to include

- Make sure that you identify the different definitions of 'being a consumer', for the purposes of UTCC Regs 1999, and 'dealing as a consumer', for the purposes of SGA 1979 and UCTA 1977.
- Be sure that you explain, with examples, the extent to which consumers are protected.
- Explain what a minority shareholder is as well as the ways in which they are protected.
- Explain the statutory rights which prevent the exploitation of employees.

✓ Make your answer stand out

Make sure that you give your opinion as to whether the protection is adequate, and make sure that you can justify your opinion with reference to the legal position. This is how the highest marks are gained. A mere opinion, without reference to the law, is of little value. Accurately describing the law will allow you to do quite well. But if the question asked for your opinion then a well-thought-out opinion, backed up by reference to the legal position, will gain the highest marks.

Glossary of terms

The glossary is divided into two parts: key definitions and other useful terms. The key definitions can be found within the chapter in which they occur as well as in the glossary below. These definitions are the essential terms that you must know and understand in order to prepare for an exam. The additional list of terms provides further definitions of useful terms and phrases which will also help you answer examination and coursework questions effectively. These terms are highlighted in the text on their first occurrence but the definition can only be found here.

Key definitions

Actionable misrepresentation	An untrue statement of fact which induced the other party to make the contract.
Agency worker	A worker who does not work directly for an employer, but does so via an employment agency.
Anticipatory breach	A breach of contract which occurs when, before performance of the contract is due, one of the parties makes it plain to the other party that the contract will not be performed.
Basic award	An amount of money to which unfairly dismissed employees are entitled.
Casting vote	An extra vote given to the chairperson of a meeting if the votes of all the members who vote are equally split.
Common mistake	A mistake which occurs when the parties to the contract reach an agreement but do so while they are both making the same fundamental mistake.
Consumer contracts	Contracts under which a trader supplier or agrees to supply goods, digital contract (software) or services to a consumer.
Contracts of sale of goods	A contract under which a buyer pays money, or promises to pay. money, in return for the ownership of goods. Goods are physical

	things which can be touched and moved. Services are not goods, nor are land or houses.
Crystallisation	The process by which a floating charge becomes a fixed charge attaching to the assets of the company which are charged at that time. When crystallisation occurs the company is no longer free to dispose of the assets.
Derivative claim	A claim brought by a member of the company to gain a remedy for the company for some wrong done to the company.
Direct discrimination	Discrimination which occurs when an employer treats a woman less favourably, on the grounds of her sex, than he would treat a man.
Dismissal (for purposes of unfair dismissal)	A dismissal occurs if: 1. the employer terminates the contract, with or without notice; 2. a fixed term contract ends and is not renewed; or 3. the employee terminates the contract on the grounds of the employer's unreasonable conduct.
Disqualification order	A court order which prevents a person from being a director, or from being concerned in the management of a company, without approval from the court.
Dividend	A payment out of the company's profits to the company members.
Employee	A person employed under a contract of employment, also known as a contract of service.
Entrenched article of association	An article that can be amended or repealed only if conditions are met, or procedures complied with, which are more restrictive than those applicable in the case of a special resolution.
Express term	A term which was expressed by the parties in words.
Fixed-term contract	A contract of employment under which it is agreed at the outset that it will exist for a fixed time, rather than being a contract which can be ended by giving notice.
Fraudulent misrepresentation	A misrepresentation which was made either knowing that it was false, or without belief in its truth or recklessly/carelessly as to whether it was true or false.
Golden rule	A rule which holds that the words of a statute should be given their ordinary, grammatical meaning as far as possible but not if this would produce an absurd result.
Implied term	A contract term which was not expressed by the parties in words.
Independent contractor	A person who makes a contract to provide a service, but does not do so as an employee.

Invitation to treat An invitation to bargain, or an invitation to make an offer. The key point is that an invitation to treat is not itself an offer.

Like work Work done by an employee which is the same or of a broadly similar nature to the work done by a person with whom the employee wishes to compare him- or herself.

Literal rule A rule which holds that the words of a statute should be given their ordinary, grammatical meaning even if this produces an absurd result.

Mischief rule A rule which allows a court to consider what mischief, or problem, the statute was passed to correct.

Negligent misrepresentation A misrepresentation made honestly believing that it was true by a person who cannot prove that he or she had reasonable grounds for this belief.

New-style memorandum of association A statement that the subscribers, the people who sign the memorandum, wish to form a company under the 2006 Act and that they agree to become members of the company by taking at least one share each.

Objects clause A clause, required to be contained in an old-style memorandum of association, which sets out the 'objects' of the company. That is to say, it set out the types of contract which the company could validly make.

Offeree A person to whom an offer has been made.

Offeror A person who makes an offer.

Ordinary resolution A resolution of company members, which is passed if more than 50% of members who vote cast their votes in favour of the resolution.

Partnership The relationship which subsists between persons carrying on a business in common with a view of profit.

Personal characteristic Under the Equality Act 2010, one of the nine grounds on which discrimination is outlawed.

Postal rule An acceptance by letter can be effective when it is posted.

Private nuisance A tort committed by a substantial, unreasonable interference with a claimant's land or with a claimant's use or enjoyment of land.

Producer of a product (for purposes of sections 1 and 2 of the CPA 1987)

- The manufacturer of the product
- The extractor of raw materials
- Industrial processors of agricultural produce
- Own branders who add their label to products which they did not produce
- Anyone who imports the product into the EU.

Pro rata principle	A principle which requires that a part-time worker should receive the appropriate proportion of pay and other benefits enjoyed by a full-time worker with whom he or she compares him- or herself.
Quorum	The minimum number of people required to be present at a meeting before the meeting can validly take place.
Ratio decidendi	A statement of law which a court applied to the facts of a case and which caused the case to be decided as it was. Usually abbreviated as the reason for the decision.
Seller or supplier (for purposes of UTCC Regs 1999)	A person who is acting for purposes relating to his or her trade, business or profession.
Share premium	An extra amount paid to a company for a share, in excess of the nominal value of the share.
Special resolution	A resolution which is passed only if at least 75% of members who vote cast their votes in favour of it.
Statement of compliance	A statement that the CA 2006 requirements as to registration of a company have been complied with.
Unfair consumer term or notice	A term in a consumer contract which, contrary to the requirement of good faith, causes a significant imbalance in the parties' rights and obligations to the detriment of the consumer.
Unilateral mistake	A mistake which occurs when only one of the parties to the contract makes a mistake.
Visitor (for purposes of OLA 1957)	Any person who comes on to premises with either the express or implied permission of the occupier.
Wholly innocent misrepresentation	A misrepresentation made honestly believing that it was true by a person who can prove that he or she had reasonable grounds for this belief.
Wrongful dismissal	A claim in contract by an employee who has been dismissed without having been given the notice to which his or her contract entitled him or her.

Other useful terms

Act of God	A defence in tort, which applies when natural forces caused the act complained of, in circumstances which no human foresight could provide against.
AGM	The annual general meeting of a company.

Comparator	A person in the same employment with whom an employee alleging certain types of discrimination must compare him- or herself.
Condition	A term which seemed vitally important when the contract was made. Breach of such a term allows the injured party to terminate the contract.
***Force majeure* clause**	A clause in a contract sets out what should happen if unexpected difficulties should arise.
Innominate (or intermediate) term	A term, breach of which will allow the injured party to terminate the contract only if he or she was 'deprived of substantially the whole benefit' of the contract.
Liquidated damages	Damages stated in the contract itself, which amount to a 'genuine pre-estimate of the loss'.
Minor	A person who is under 18 years of age.
Nominal damages	Token damages.
Non est factum	A kind of mistake which makes a contract void because a person, who was not careless, was completely mistaken about the nature of what he or she signed.
Obiter dicta	Statements of law made by a court which do not amount to the *ratio decidendi* of the case.
Penalty	A large sum, set out in a contract as the amount of damages payable in the event of breach, which is not liquidated damages because it is not a 'genuine pre-estimate of the loss'.
Privity	A doctrine that a contract is private between the parties who created it, so that it cannot be enforced by anyone else nor can it impose a burden on anybody else.
Quantum meruit	A claim for payment of the amount deserved for work done.
Strict liability	Liability which arises without fault.
Volenti non fit injuria	A defence to an action in tort, whereby the defendant shows that the claimant voluntarily assumed the risk which caused his or her injury.
Warranty	A term which did not seem vitally important when the contract was made. Breach of a warranty does not allow the injured party to terminate the contract.

Index